THE CAPACITY
MODEL

How to Build Your Best Life

STEVE PERRY

To my wife, Tabatha.

A woman who inspires me every day with her drive

to grow her own capacity, as well as that of everyone around her.

Table of Contents

Introduction 1

Part 1: *The Capacity Model* 5

    Chapter 1: The Honeymoon 6

    Chapter 2: Time To Grow 11

    Chapter 3: The Capacity Model 15

    Chapter 4: Breakdown Or Breakthrough 17

    Chapter 5: Four Truths To Follow 22

Part 2: *Education* 30

    Chapter 6: Formal Education 32

    Chapter 7: Informal Education 39

Part 3: *Habits* 69

    Chapter 8: "Being" Habits 71

    Chapter 9: "Relating" Habits 84

    Chapter 10: "Doing" Habits 99

Part 4: *Relationships* 114

    Chapter 11: Professional Relationships 116

    Chapter 12: Personal Relationships 123

Part 5: *Breakthrough* 137

    Chapter 13: Closing Thoughts 139

Acknowledgments 141

About The Author...143

Introduction

"Stress is a gift…"

Reed's voice echoed in my head. The matter-of-fact way he stated the words made me wonder if he realized the irony laced in them. My default was to believe him because he was my business coach, and frankly, I had never been able to prove him wrong.

"Stress is life's natural gift telling you it's time to grow!"

That explanation was a little less ironic. It was beginning to make sense. I was worn out from growth.

Our organization had experienced exponential growth at a level seldom seen for a single office inside our Fortune 100 financial services firm. I had arrived a little more than two years earlier to assume command as the managing partner of our little office in West Texas.

There are typically two ways you come into an office. First, the former leader messed up so badly that he or she got fired/demoted/transferred. You are blessed with the gift of cleaning up the mess and trying and make something of the wreckage. The second scenario is that the former leader was so successful in cleaning up wreckage in the past that he or she was promoted to a bigger and better office, and your job is not to screw up what you've been handed.

My arrival was based on the latter premise. The office had doubled in size over the previous four years. My assignment was clear: *do not screw it up!*

Not only did we not screw it up; we repeated the results. We doubled the office's size and production in less than three years. We were on a roll!

Notice, I say "we." It was an enormous team effort.

Notice, I say "team." We truly operated like one.

We spent every day together. We could count on each other to cover duties. We bounced ideas off each other all the time. We worked hard, had fun. It was amazing! This was the type of team you set out to build when you draw it up. Sure, we weren't perfect, but our blind spots led to growth opportunities. And when you are winning, it makes everything even more worth it.

That is why I was caught so off-guard that January morning. I had it all planned out. I had arranged for *Twelve-Week Year* author Brian Moran to visit and do a workshop with our entire organization. The hope was to install the Twelve-Week Year system into our organization and start implementing his techniques. He had been scheduled to do biweekly calls with our leadership team to help capitalize on the momentum we had and to catapult us to the next level. I had scheduled the initial intake call, which was to take place later that day.

It *did not* go well. In fact, one might describe it as a small revolt. One by one, the entire leadership team told me why they thought this was a terrible idea and how they were offended that I had suggested they needed an outside coach. Wasn't that *my* job? Did I believe they weren't performing well enough?

And my favorite, "Who is this *Brian* guy?"

Epic fail.

I had spent weeks putting this strategy together, connecting with the author, coordinating conference calls, and talking myself into spending the money. All this was to help them grow—to help *us* grow. Isn't that what we all wanted? I thought so, at least. But that didn't stop this miniature mutiny from happening. I didn't understand it. I wasn't sure how I was going to build confidence in the team again and right this ship. We were coming off an incredibly successful year to beat, and we were now listing in the wrong direction.

Desperate, I called Reed, and that's when he told me, "Stress is a gift."

Part 1: The Capacity Model

One definition of *capacity* in Merriam-Webster's dictionary is "an individual's mental or physical ability (aptitude, skill)." Another is "the potential for treating, experiencing, or appreciating" something, such as success or love.

Capacity is the foundation of a framework I use that enables us to build our best lives; I call it "the Capacity Model."

The Capacity Model is predicated on a universal truth that we all experience stress. It explains our current ability and future potential to handle all the challenges and opportunities that life throws at us. When we do not handle difficulties well, we experience stress, which can be quite damaging to our well-being over time.

To increase our threshold for experiencing stress, we have to understand the three components of the Capacity Model—education, habits, and relationships—and increase our effectiveness in each of these areas. Doing so will enable us to minimize our stress levels and enhance our quality of life.

Chapter 1: The Honeymoon

"Where do you want to go to dinner?" Joe asked his new bride, Sarah, on the first night of their honeymoon.

They had just settled into their hotel room, and Sarah was smiling. "I don't care, wherever you want, honey."

"Okay, let's go to The Cheesecake Factory," Joe said quickly. He began envisioning all the menu options that were sure to please both of them.

"Nah, I don't really want to go there. There are too many decisions to make. Let's go somewhere else."

Joe's eyebrows pinched in question. "But you just said you didn't care." He immediately regretted his retort.

Sarah sighed. "I've had a long day. We've been on the plane for hours, and I just want to go somewhere low-key. I'm sure it will be packed with people anyway, and we'll have a long wait—"

"Obviously, you have something better in mind, so let's just go there." The somewhat snarky response spewed out of Joe's mouth before his brain could throw up the warning sign of "bad idea."

"I don't, actually." She grabbed the keys and headed toward the rental car. "You know what? Let's just go there. I don't want to argue about it."

Even though Joe got the restaurant of his choice, it certainly didn't feel like he'd "won." His frustration built up. Where had this version of Sarah come from? She made no logical sense—full of contradictions. They had been married less than twenty-four hours, and he was already starting to wonder if he had been too hasty in marrying her. The stress of marriage had already encompassed their relationship.

They arrived at the restaurant, and—just as Sarah had expected—it was packed. The hostess stated it would be a forty-five-minute wait to be seated, but if they could find a seat at the bar, they were welcome to it. Rather than deal with Sarah's wrath and attempt to decide on a new venue, Joe spotted two high-top chairs and waved Sarah over.

They both ordered a cocktail to numb the stress of their earlier argument. Sarah ordered a gin–martini, and Joe ordered an old-fashioned. As they scoured the voluminous menu for something that would satisfy their hunger, the waiter brought them their drinks.

"I'll have the Asian chicken salad, but instead of chicken can I have shrimp?" Sarah ordered.

"Absolutely," the waiter responded.

"Great! Make sure the tails are cut off the shrimp. I would like them blackened, please, *not* grilled. And if you could have the dressing come on the side that would be great. Also, if you could only use spinach in the salad, I would appreciate it. And if you can split it and bring half out on the plate and the other half in a to go container, I can save the rest for tomorrow."

If Joe's energy hadn't already been depleted, that did the trick. "I'll just have the bacon cheeseburger," he said.

The couple barely spoke as they sipped their drinks and observed the commotion surrounding them. Joe braced for Sarah's pending fit caused by the cooks inevitably messing up her complex order. Why did she have to be so picky?

Miraculously, their food came just as ordered and they quickly ate.

As the bill came, Joe handed his credit card to Sarah and asked her to pay the bill while he went to the restroom. Upon return, Sarah had just slung her purse over her shoulder, ready to head back to their hotel.

"Did we get the bill paid?" Joe asked.

"Nope, I thought we would dine and dash," Sarah smiled jokingly as she pointed to the signed receipt on the table.

Joe's laughter faded as he glanced at the receipt while walking toward the door.

Food/Beverage: $57.94

Tip: $5.00

Total: $62.94

Something didn't seem right. "Sarah, did you know you left less than a 10% tip?" Joe asked as they slithered through the crowd and out the front door.

"Well yeah," Sarah replied incredulously. "Why would I leave more than that?"

Joe's mind raced to recall any time during their dating or engagement where Sarah had paid for a meal. He couldn't locate a single memory of this in their short past together. His ire from before returned.

He had married a 10 percent tipper! His many years in the restaurant industry had caused him to loathe these selfish misers. Didn't they realize that the servers planned their families' budgets based on a customary gratuity nearing twice that amount? And now he was eternally bonded with one of these people whom he vowed never to associate with.

The life of a bachelor seemed mighty fine in that moment. The stress from earlier again caused him to ponder the mistake he may have made by marrying this woman. Had he really made a mistake?

The silence on the drive home became deafening. Joe's mind raced. His knuckles whitened on the steering wheel. Sarah sat there, clueless to Joe's disdain for her.

They arrived at the hotel and rode the elevator up to their room. Because of a reservation blunder, the newlyweds found themselves in a romantic room equipped with two full-size beds. Less than the idyllic "Honeymoon Suite" they had envisioned.

As they prepared for bed, Sarah casually stated, "I am feeling pretty tired tonight, babe. I know it's the first night of our honeymoon, but I would really like to just go straight to bed. We have six more nights here anyway."

Joe halted, his toothbrush dangling from his mouth. He couldn't believe the words he just heard. Was this a bad dream?

He spewed the foamy toothpaste from his mouth. "Ha! I shouldn't even be surprised after how tonight's already gone. You know, it's a good thing they gave us two separate beds. I hope you enjoy sleeping by yourself tonight."

He marched over to his bed, threw back the covers, slid under the sheets, and rolled onto his side with his back to her, staring at the wall next to him.

Joe couldn't sleep. His mind kept replaying the first twenty-four hours of their marital non-bliss. The indecision about the restaurant. The meticulous, high-maintenance food order, and that lousy excuse for a server's tip. Then finally, the absence of their first night of honeymoon sex. The dam hadn't just cracked, it had overflowed.

In just a few short hours, Joe had experienced the first two phases of breakdown in the Capacity Model. His disappointment had graduated beyond disillusionment, and he considered how to undo this obvious mistake. This is not what he had envisioned for his best life.

Chapter 2: Time to Grow

Again, the Capacity Model is predicated on a universal truth: that we all experience stress. Many of us are conditioned to view stress from a negative perspective. We do everything we can to avoid it, yet everyone still experiences it.

The concept I am introducing to you is one I have been taught: *stress is a gift.* Stress is life's natural gift. It provides us with an opportunity to challenge ourselves. It tells us, "Hey, it's time to grow!"

As we progress through life, our ability to handle stress varies widely, depending on our capacity for stress in that moment. Although not always true, typically, our capacity grows throughout our lifetime as we encounter newer and higher levels of stressful experiences.

Remember high-school finals week? We could not fathom how we could possibly survive all our exams. We were stressed about the future being solely dependent on our grades. We stressed out if one of our teachers added something to an exam that we hadn't really studied that much, as if it was the end of the world.

I complained to my parents about how busy of a week it had been. Gracious as they were, they said, "Steve, don't worry. You'll get through this!" They were smiling, as if their advice was the most logical thing in the world.

The reason it was so stressful was because my fourteen-year-old capacity could only handle so much.

As we learn to navigate life's challenges, we become more adept at dealing with stress. As I grew and matured throughout life, I was able handle more and more...and more:

- Shooting game ending free-throws in the state basketball tournament
- Getting my first job
- Deciding which colleges to apply to
- *Not* getting into that one college I applied to
- Figuring out how to pay for college
- Coming out of college realizing I would have to pay back those loans
- Landing my first real job
- Planning my wedding
- Getting married
- Becoming a parent.
- Leading my first team
- Leading an entire organization

If you take the time to reflect on these different stages in your life, I am sure they will trigger some exciting and fond memories. Many of them do for me.

Then, if you reflect a second time, you might even physically relive the deep stress and anxiety these situations initially caused you. If you are like most people, you chalk it up to "This is just life" or "I am just paying my dues." While those scenarios could be true, I find it is much more constructive to identify what can be gleaned from every "negative" experience in life and do whatever is within my ability to avoid experiencing the same results from the same methods again.

In our example from before, Joe encountered his first experience of stress that comes from being married to another human being. And I encountered stress with change management, coming off a win with a newly developed leadership team. Both situations are complex. Both are specific.

Unlocking the key to handling stress, so you can build your best life, lies within The Capacity Model.

Chapter 3: The Capacity Model

Our capacity is built on three personal-development pillars that all of us stand on in everyday life. Each of them is *independent*, meaning that we can develop them independently of the others and our capacity will grow. They are also *interdependent*, meaning that if we combine enhancements in all three areas together, we get an exponential growth curve in our total capacity.

Think of your capacity as a triangle-shaped canopy. Three pillars hold up this canopy. Each of these pillar's relative height is based on the amount of development you have put into it. The more time you have devoted to bettering your progress into the disciplines—and specifically, how effective you have been—the taller the pillar is. This, in turn, pushes the ceiling of the canopy up higher in the corresponding corner. If one area has a lower ceiling than the other, that doesn't mean you don't have sufficient overall capacity. It does mean that if you raised up that pillar, you would have a more balanced capacity, and it would take a lot more to cause stress.

It's a simple but powerful model. There are only three pillars:

- Education
- Habits
- Relationships

Your current level of education, habits, and relationships establishes the ceiling of your capacity.

As we go through life, many of us are running hard to *get stuff done*. We have been raised to think that this is a noble pursuit. It is engrained in us as *The American Dream*—work hard, get rewarded! The problem is that this approach inevitably causes us to hit our heads against our capacity ceiling. You'll know when you've hit that ceiling because you can feel the stress.

Chapter 4: Breakdown or Breakthrough

When the stress of maxing out our current capacity starts to permeate our lives, the amygdala in the brain starts to take over, and we start to make imprudent decisions. Emotional Intelligence experts refer to this as *amygdala hijacking*. In other words, you start to break down.

Depending on the situation, this can be a quick breakdown that leads to devastating results. An example of this would be a commission-based sales professional who is behind in his numbers. After work, he tries to numb out by having too many drinks at the bar. Then he makes the poor decision of getting behind the wheel and driving. From there, the consequences tend to get severe and potentially permanent—all within a twenty-four-hour period.

Three Stages of a Breakdown

Let's take a closer look at how the standard breakdown model presents itself. This is a drastic and atypical example of how a breakdown happens, but it demonstrates the three stages well. The three stages are: disappointment, disillusionment, and greener pastures.

For this model, we will follow the story of Chuck. Chuck is a recently promoted Regional Vice President to a new territory. He is excited about his new role, which he quickly learns is incredibly more complex than his prior experience of running a small team.

1. Disappointment

When Chuck arrives at his new location, he quickly learns that he has inherited an extremely talented and autonomous team. No matter what he does, it seems like he cannot get his new team to follow his lead. To them, he is just another guy in the office.

Chuck is experiencing the first stage of breakdown: *disappointment.* He had been excited and optimistic about the promise of his new role. However, his eager anticipation of what his new role could be has been erased. He comes home each day, trying to determine what went wrong and why he isn't getting the results he wants.

A dark, negative cloud looms over him, and the harder he tries to force things to happen, the more they seem to go sideways. His amygdala takes over, and he succumbs to his anxiety, deciding, "*It's my way or no way*" with his new team. Bad move, Chuck.

As he continues to delve deeper into an autocratic style of leadership and grab a firmer grip of those on his team, things get worse. They stop collaborating with each other. In fact, they stop communicating altogether. Factions are created inside the organization, and battle lines are drawn. All this is caused by the negative repercussions of Chuck's chosen leadership style.

2. Disillusionment

As the situation worsens, Chuck enters stage two of breakdown. He becomes *disillusioned*.

Internally, at first, he asks himself why he ever accepted this promotion. Life would have been so much better if he just stayed put in his previous position. Could he go back to that role and save face?

Eventually, he starts to say these things out loud. It first comes out to his wife after a few beers on a Friday night. Then they talk about it more extensively. Next, it slips out with some friends. Now the cat is out of the bag. Because Chuck finds himself verbalizing his disillusionment, he believes he is the victim and that he is owed the option to recant his acceptance of the new role. As a result, he brings up the subject to his superiors.

3. The Desire to Find Greener Pastures

Like toothpaste, once you squeeze it out of the tube, it's not going back in there. The comment to his superiors has been made, and Chuck's bosses start the process of moving him back to where he came from. Chuck is getting exactly what he thinks he wants. That is because he has moved on to the final stage of breakdown: *greener pastures*.

It looks better, it smells better, it tastes better, and ultimately, it seems better—this backward movement. That is why people in the final stage of breakdown compromise all their goals, aspirations, dreams, and desires to make a move that they never would have considered. They don't realize that the real problem is that *their capacity had not been built up enough* to handle the stressful experiences that life was presenting them.

Greener pastures feel good for a while. I have witnessed greener-pasture transitions dozens of times in my career. It deeply saddens me when I see people leave their promising careers when it starts to get hard. They move on to a new position that is "easier," and they give up on their long-term aspirations.

What Can Happen when You Transition into "Greener Pastures"

It's important to understand what happens with the model as you shift into a *greener pasture* position. Typically, the new role is significantly under your capacity ceiling. Think of this as being extremely overqualified for the position.

The problem is that the world is constantly evolving and growing. Because of this, if you transition into a *greener pasture*, then over time, you will ultimately hit that capacity celling again. You will start to feel stress. That stress will build until you come to a breaking point. And if you don't follow the steps to breakthrough, you will probably experience another breakdown. The continuous cycle of breakdown is vicious and pervasive. If you enter it, you will move from greener pasture to greener pasture in search of relief from stress. You will never find it, though. This is because you have done nothing to address your ultimate capacity. Instead, you have just put yourself in a position that places you under your capacity ceiling.

I think it is important to pause here and defend Chuck. Although he made some poor decisions and didn't choose to move toward breakthrough, all of us have been guilty of this in our lives. Big or small, we have all been presented with stressful situations in which we have decidedly gone down the path of breakdown and ended up choosing the greener pasture.

This could be as simple as ending an argument with the words, "Fine, you do it your way!"

Or it could be as complex as re-uprooting your family to take a demotion so that life isn't so stressful. We have all experienced breakdowns. And that is OK because it is the cycle of breakdown that gives you the opportunity to choose the alternate path: *breakthrough!*

Let's revisit Chuck's story. Imagine that instead of succumbing to his frustration when he realized that things were not going his way and that he and his team weren't connecting, he reached out for help. Let's say he realized that his capacity ceiling was low and that he needed to change that.

Fortunately, he had some good *relationships* with people whom he could be transparent with and ask for help.

Grow in Three Areas

Relationships, education, and habits are *the pillars* in creating breakthrough.

Larry was not only Chuck's boss, but also his mentor. Chuck had known Larry for a long time, and it was Larry who brought him into the company in the first place. Although they had lost touch in recent months, Chuck knew he needed to rekindle this relationship. Certainly, Larry could help him figure out why this wasn't working. He called Larry.

During this call, Larry introduced Chuck to the Capacity Model. Larry explained that the reason Chuck was feeling stressed out was because he was hitting his head on his personal-capacity ceiling. He had two choices: *breakdown* or *breakthrough*.

Larry told Chuck, "To have a breakthrough, it is not going to be an easy or painless experience. It's going to be hard. But it will produce the long-term results you want."

What Chuck needed to do was grow. Specifically, he needed to grow in three areas: *education, habits,* and *relationships.*

Larry told Chuck, "If you are truly open to growing, to committing in your mind to develop in any one of these areas and take the actions necessary to implement that growth, you will increase your capacity ceiling. And if you choose to grow in all three areas, you will significantly increase your capacity ceiling and begin to *handle stress so you can live your best life!*"

Chapter 5: Four Truths to Follow

Before we examine the components of building your capacity, it's important to understand four different truths that will help you accomplish this. Each of these truths is born from excuses I have heard others tell themselves. These excuses either impede the breakthrough process or cause you to enter the breakdown cycle.

To break away from old patterns, work on transforming those excuses into four truths to follow.

1. Whether You Do or Don't Is Up to You

The first truth you must accept is that whether you grow is up to you. It is imperative that you adopt this mindset of *determinism*—a theory that says acts of the will, occurrences in nature, or social or psychological phenomena are causally determined by preceding events or natural laws.

It is up to you to take control of your attitude and your activity. Your attitude sets your *altitude*—how high you can go, and your activity sets your *amplitude*—how big you make it.

I recently began sending out a series of messages to some of my social media connections. It is a set of affirmations that I wrote to help encourage others. They go like this:

- Laura is a powerful creator.
- Jeff is courageous.
- Ryan has everything needed to face any obstacle.

- Abby crushes goals.
- Be encouraged today! You bring incredible value to this world!

For years, I didn't grasp the power of affirmations. What I realize now is that they silence the fear and doubt that creeps into our lives, telling us we can't do something. There is always a voice going on in our heads. It is up to us to tell ourselves we *can* accomplish something. And when we do, we are right.

2. Limitations Manifest in All Aspects of Our lives

As human beings, we are whole people. We cannot separate portions of our lives effectively for very long. This is why I am not a fan of the phrase "work–life balance." I think that whenever possible, we should strive to integrate our work and personal lives to work together and to drive our purpose.

When you reach your capacity ceiling, your whole life is stressed out. If you are stressed at work, your kids and spouse will not get your best self. If you are maxed out at home, you will be at a disadvantage leading your team.

The optimistic side of me chooses to call out the other side of the coin. When you grow your education, habits, and relationships; your personal and professional capacity improves as well. You will be not only a better employee, leader, and business owner; you will be a better friend, spouse, parent, and community member.

There is so much to gain in our whole life by choosing to expand our capacity. I implore you to realize the whole picture of your life as you are going through this book. As you do this, you will notice that you are becoming a better person throughout your whole life.

3. Life Is *Hard*

Ouch! How's that for discouraging? It's a harsh reality: life is *hard*. We have all experienced the difficulties that life throws at us. I believe all things work together for good. When life is challenging, it is up to us to choose what we do about it.

With regard to capacity building, it's important to recognize your choices.

The first version of the concept that "life is hard," as I previously mentioned, is to enter the breakdown cycle. Divorce, resignation, and estrangement are drastic examples—nasty consequences that result from allowing stress to overtake us and not choosing to grow. These are extremely hard circumstances to endure, and people don't typically choose them willfully. Often, the breakdown cycle is a result of *apathy*. The hard truth is, apathy is a choice.

When we bury our heads in the sand, remain indifferent toward our stress, and wallow in it, we are actively choosing to head down these tough roads. There are consequences associated with apathy, and they will rear their ugly heads. Take a moment to travel down the road of what your conscious indecision will lead to. Feel that pain. Channel it toward breakthrough.

Breakthrough is our alternative to breakdown. Breakthrough, our second version of "life is hard," evokes a conquering image of an athlete or warrior, but the journey that gets you there is also full of pain and difficulty. Many times, as you toil to establish new habits, struggle to learn new concepts, or experience rejection in new relationships, you will think, "Wow, this is hard!" And you will be right.

Growth is not easy, or everyone would do it. Sometimes that pain comes from not seeing growth, despite the discipline you are exerting. Remind yourself that giving up will not get you anywhere. You are already in pain; you might as well get a prize for it—in the form of expanded capacity.

I find it is helpful to anticipate that it will not be easy so that when you endure the anguish of progress, you are not caught off-guard. You have hopefully built a framework of supporting relationships around you to encourage and support you on this continuous excursion because, after all, your best life is waiting!

4. Doing More ≠ Working More Hours

Finally, I must correct a common myth: embarking on this quest to expand your capacity does not mean you are working more hours.

I find that often, people resign themselves to just spending more time "doing." While there are seasons for this, by the very nature that you have taken it upon yourself to read this book, I am going to assume you are already a doer and work hard by nature.

It is important to understand that your 168 hours each week are already spoken for. You have allocated them and have been allocating them since the beginning of your life. I will explain how to deliberately plan them later in this book; however, I want to start right now by saying this: *do not work more hours.*

Use the Pareto Principle to Your Advantage

Instead, abide by the Pareto principle, also called the 80–20 rule. it says that 80 percent of our results come from 20 percent of our activities. My experience says that this scales even further, and I like to take it to the third degree.

Here is an example that helps explain this principle.

Let's say you worked 100 hours one week, and you were able to make $100 in those hours. (Yes, that's only $1 per hour, but I want the math to be simple here.)

According to the Pareto principle, there are 20 hours in that week that would account for $80 of your revenue.

Now, 20 percent of those 20 hours (4 hours) will provide 80 percent of the $80, which is $64. That means there are 4 hours in your week that provide $64 of your revenue.

Now do that calculation one more time. Twenty percent of those 4 hours is $\approx$ 1 hour that will create 80 percent of your $64, which is approximately $50.

In other words, if you apply the Pareto principle three times, you will realize that 1 percent of your activity will lead to 50 percent of your results.

Here's the math:

Activities:

20% X 20% X 20% = 0.8%

Results:

80% X 80% X 80% = 51.2%

Here's an example to help clarify how this works.

Jim is a new financial advisor. As a fledgling business owner, he has multiple competing priorities each day. Many seem urgent, but only a few are important. (I define *important* as directly contributing to revenue because a business must generate money to continue running.)

Let's say Jim works 50 hours per week and makes $100,000 annually. He spends 10 hours each week sitting in front of prospective clients, conducting planning meetings. The Pareto principle says this specific activity that Jim spends 10 hours on each week (20% of his activities) will lead to $80,000 of his annual income (80% of results).

We can scale that down even further if we apply the Pareto principle again.

Let's say Jim spends 2 hours each week conducting planning meetings with highly qualified, *ideal* prospective clients. Those 2 hours represent 20% of Jim's 10 hours of activities each week and produce $64,000 of Jim's annual income (80% of the $80,0000).

Finally, we can scale that down one more time. There are 24 minutes each week (20% of the 2 hours) that produce $51,200 of Jim's annual income (80% of the $64,000). Better yet, for 1.5 hours each month (4 x 24 minutes), Jim is sitting in front of highly qualified, *ideal* prospective clients conducting the implementation of (closing) a financial plan.

The takeaway for Jim here is that he needs to build an infrastructure (technology and employees) and systems (standard operating procedures) in his company that put him in a position to do "high-return" activities as often as possible. This will help him maximize his results.

To restate, roughly 1 percent of your activities produce roughly 50 percent of your results. Identify those activities that will have the biggest impact on your capacity. Then in any given week, you need to spend only 90 minutes (~1 percent of 168 hours per week) doing them to get huge results.

If you approach this book with the mindset of not doing more but doing better, you will grow your capacity exponentially. And you will get there more quickly than you can imagine. This is why CEOs of large companies can be led by younger, less-tenured people or why, at times, it doesn't' matter how many "years in the business" top salespeople or athletes have. They have mastered the science of determining what is most important and then allocating their time effectively.

It might take some time, initially, to determine what this looks like for you. Begin by identifying the biggest levers in improving your education, habits, and relationships first, you will be able to do it without a long-term increase in hours spent.

Isn't that a component of all of our best lives...the time to spend as we choose?

Part 2: Education

What do you think of when you hear the word *education*? For some people, it conjures up images of sitting at a desk in grade school, passing notes, throwing spit wads at other students, and playing pranks on substitute teachers.

Then you move on to where it all starts to count: high school.

That's when you get report cards that count toward your overall grade-point average (GPA), which is now part of your "permanent record." Then comes college, where eighteen-year-olds are supposed to figure out what they want to do for the rest of their lives. If you get it wrong, the penalty is thousands or even hundreds of thousands of dollars down the drain. And if you got a loan to pay for that tuition, you *get* to pay interest on that mistake as well.

This is not necessarily the type of education that builds your capacity in life. It's not really important whether you know how to correctly spell "misspell" or how to figure out what 2,213 divided by 13 equals by doing long division by hand. That kind of education does not increase your capacity ceiling.

However, the education you receive while spending time in school does have a lot to do with your capacity. What contributes most to your capacity are not the factoids you learn. Rather, what builds your capacity in school are social interactions you have, the emotional intelligence you build, the stamina and grit you demonstrate, and the self-discipline and teamwork you build. These experiences will increase your ability to handle stress throughout your lifetime.

So, specifically, what type of education is going to help you build your capacity? What are the components, and what can you do to maximize this pillar?

Ultimately, education can be broken down into two subcategories: *formal* and *informal.* Let's explore what these are and what you can do to experience growth in both areas.

Chapter 6: Formal Education

Did you have to write a check for your college tuition? Was there a syllabus that described what your education would look like? How about a piece of paper saying "You learned!" (a diploma) when you graduated? If so, then you experienced formal education.

In the context of building capacity, it is important to identify the components of education that are helpful. Although you learn many things while going through formal education, not everything builds capacity. Once we identify the elements that do, you can begin to identify commonalities and then be intentional about seeking out this education in your everyday life.

High School: The Beginning of Stress for Many People

Our first exposure to formal education on a somewhat professional scale is high school. The lockers, the bells, the class schedule, dating, sports—oh, yeah, and the school part. There is a lot of potential to build capacity in high school. Some of the first stress many people recall happen in high school.

I can recall several times going into finals week and not having any idea how I was going to get through it. I had dozens of pages of papers to write for books I hadn't even cracked, formulas to memorize for chemistry classes, and most importantly, playing in basketball tournaments.

You see, the capacity lessons you learn in your formal high school education have more to do with the prioritizing and calendaring of activities, learning, studying, participating in athletics, and socializing, than they do with the periodic table of elements.

The following are a few areas students tend to focus on in high school: GPA, extracurricular activities, and social interactions. Let's look at each one.

1. GPA

Your grade point average (GPA) is important for one reason only: it gets you into the college you were supposed to get into, or it doesn't. Either way, you have the ability to grow by learning the material teachers present to you, but your GPA establishes one of the first marks in your life that helps determine what big decision to make next.

If you have a high GPA, it creates more capacity for you to go into a more competitive and high-achieving environment. In this environment, your capacity ceiling will be put to the test more quickly, and you will be forced to continue to grow. If you have a low GPA, you probably won't have the best options, and you will be forced to grow in a different way. You will have to "come from behind" to increase your capacity and ultimately reach your potential.

Either way works. Either way has just as much potential.

2. Extracurricular Activities

Extracurricular activities—those you participate in outside the regular track of education—are extremely important in capacity building. Consistent participation in clubs and on teams shows you have decided to add more to your plate. And doing *more* always gives you an opportunity to grow. Remember, you can grow your capacity ceiling by increasing each of the pillars holding up that ceiling. Whenever you pursue the pillar of education, your capacity grows.

Extracurricular activities allow you to learn how to prioritize competing demands. You get to select what specific skill sets you want to develop (versus the mandatory classes that everyone is required to take). All these decisions and interactions contribute toward creating who you will become.

3. Social Interactions

Building your social circle in high school can be a painful process. Many people experience an incredible amount of stress in high school around their social encounters. This gives way to the Capacity Model because it gives people initial opportunities to choose breakdown or breakthrough.

You learn what works and what doesn't. You learn how hard you are willing to try to *fit in*, or you choose not to. You establish your personal values and integrity and prepare yourself to build Version 2.0 of yourself: College You.

College: Your Choices Create Long-Term Implications

College is a formidable time in people's lives, for many reasons. According to the Bureau of Labor Statistics, of the 3.2 million people ages 16 to 24 who graduated from high school between January and October 2019, 2.1 million—66.2 percent—were enrolled in colleges or universities in October 2019.[1] Most of us have potential capacity built around education in college. This is where your formal education really takes off, to create long-term implications about your capacity. This is true particularly if you are becoming a professional who is required to have a degree or certification from a school to become licensed, such as a doctor, lawyer, nurse, engineer, or architect.

Although you might not know what you want to do for your career when entering college, at some point, you have to decide and start heading down a path. This can cause some stress. Most people begin by taking general education classes, which offer introductions to many different areas of study. This exposure can influence the direction of your education. Regardless, you will be faced with many new challenges that create educational opportunities.

Three of those challenges are tuition, your schedule, and social interactions (just like in high school). Let's look at each challenge.

---

1. "66.2 Percent of 2019 High School Graduates Enrolled in College in October 2019," US Bureau of Labor Statistics, May 22, 2020, https://www.bls.gov/opub/ted/2020/66-point-2-percent-of-2019-high-school-graduates-enrolled-in-college-in-october-2019.htm.

1. Tuition

Surprise—you must pay for school! There are many ways to pay for it, and each one comes with a learning curve. Scholarships, loans, grants, parents, cash—all sources have their pros and cons. Learning how to get this done can create much knowledge. The way you go about it will be evidence of the type of person you will become.

I used a combination of scholarships and cash. Based on my high-school experience, I was able to get a full-ride Naval ROTC scholarship. I quickly learned that a career in the US Navy was not the correct career path (despite my father being a retired Lieutenant Commander). I learned an extreme sense of respect for those who serve our country, but my entrepreneurial, self-motivated makeup did not bode well in the systematic structure of the Navy.

Paying $50,000 a year for school was also not something I wanted to do, so I transferred back home to the University of Alaska Anchorage (go Seawolves?) and focused on getting my degree. The process of running my own construction company in the summer, combined with working at character-building jobs at the post office and as a janitor allowed me to pay cash all the way through college. Plus, I learned humility and business at the same time.

2. Your Schedule

Even though there are people whose job it is to help you set up your class schedule and graduate on time, it simply isn't that easy. When you build your plan to graduate, you learn how to organize your priorities, conduct research, communicate, and manage your calendar.

This logistical endeavor can test the skills of even the most seasoned planner. Much of this effort translates into building your capacity through education and gives you valuable skills in life that present real-world value.

3. Social Interactions

College is where you get your first do-over. No one knows you or your history. You get to reinvent yourself. You get to proactively choose how you present yourself and then analyze responses from others. You choose the level of charisma, optimism, extroversion that you portray. You craft your stance on politicking, your tolerance for relationships, and begin professionally networking. You get betrayed, adored, praised, gossiped about, and then you choose how to react. These situations don't disappear throughout the rest of your life, and later they come with more severe consequences.

Graduate School: An Effective Opportunity to Become a Specialist

The Bureau of Labor Statistics has reported that between 2000 and 2019, the percentage of Americans with a master's or higher degree increased from 5 to 9 percent.[2] Completing a graduate degree can be an effective way to increase your capacity. Graduate degree programs are best embarked upon once you have

---

2. Fast Facts: Educational Attainment, National Center for Education Statistics (NCES), https://nces.ed.gov/fastfacts/display.asp?id=27.

a strong level of clarity for the direction in which you want to take your career.

All the learning points from undergraduate college programs apply here as well, only in a more condensed format. While programs vary widely, you are going to learn how to specialize in the career path you are headed toward. Most programs end with an in-depth practicum, thesis, or dissertation that requires hundreds, sometimes thousands of hours of practice and research learning your subject matter. The knowledge you gain while completing this advanced degree will enable you to make substantial progress in growing the pillar of *education* in your capacity.

Professional Licensing: Increase Your Capacity and Credibility

According to the Bureau of Labor Statistics, in 2018, 24.1 percent of employed Americans held an active certification or license. for their jobs.[3] While the difficulty in obtaining these certifications varies from field to field, all of them entail a certain amount of education.

Imagine the stress a first-day phlebotomist would experience if he or she didn't go through any training or certification prior to starting in the new role. Or consider the havoc wreaked by a financial advisor who has never cracked a book or passed an exam pertaining to how the stock market works.

---

3. "Professional Certifications and Occupational Licenses: Evidence from the Current Population Survey," Bureau of Labor Statistics, June 2019, https://www.bls.gov/opub/mlr/2019/article/professional-certifications-and-occupational-licenses.htm.

If you feel like your capacity is limited in the formal education realm, often, the quickest and most effective means of growing it is to get professionally licensed in your field. Many professionals, such as lawyers and engineers, have to complete some sort of test, with the capstone of gaining a license. But many other professions offer credentials you can gain to increase your capacity as well as your professional credibility.

Go for it! Get licensed! Get certified! Increase your knowledge and capacity through education—however you achieve it, your best life is waiting!

Chapter 7: Informal Education

We just spent the last few pages reviewing the types of formal education you can pursue to grow your capacity. I hope this book encourages you to take a stroll down memory lane. Perhaps you didn't realize all the capacity you were building while gaining your formal education.

Thankfully, some of it is mandated, or else we might not have chosen to engage in it. Much of the rest of it has become socially mandated, and if you are like me, you entered college without a real plan. Regardless, you are a product—or rather, your *capacity* is a product—of the formal education you acquired through the years.

Now, although the types of formal education we've discussed are important, I believe we proactively increase our capacity over our lifetimes through the informal education we achieve. *Informal education* is the microlearning that we accomplish as we navigate life. While it often occurs unwittingly, the more we learn about it and are conscious that we are gaining education in our everyday lives, the more ingrained it becomes, and the more we maximize the growth of our capacity.

When you start to feel stress, it is necessary to seek out education and apply it to achieve the breakthrough you are looking for. You don't have to read an entire book or take an entire class to experience a breakthrough. Often, it takes only a simple line in a book or a quote from a podcast to lead you to the breakthrough you need.

The cost of informal education is minimal, and the time investment is worth it, but it's up to you to seek it out. Let's look at some of the areas of everyday life in which you can proactively build your informal education.

The School of Hard Knocks

We all have faced challenges in life. Some of us were dealt a better start than others. Some people have even been dealt a hand that statistically doomed them from the start. I was blessed to live in a loving household with two parents who cared for me and gave me every opportunity they could while modeling what a loving marriage looked like. Having these advantages was wonderful, but the more difficult times in my life taught me the most and prepared me to excel in any scenario.

So much has been written on focusing on the things you can control in life. One of the beliefs in our organization is that you can control only your attitude and your activity. What influences your capacity, however, is *how you react when life seems unfair.*

My Wife's Difficult Work Situation

When my wife, Tabatha, was working for the state government in the Office of Children Services, her job was to review cases in which children, who had been given a rough lot in life from the beginning, had to enter the custody of the state. In her reviews, her role was to determine whether the state followed predetermined policy and procedure. As if this wasn't an emotional enough experience, her supervisor was nothing short of the stereotype of a horrible boss. She would pick apart Tabatha's work and give her only negative feedback on the most minute of mistakes. She would give her impossible deadlines and change protocol in the middle of assignments. The culture was toxic. Tabatha had an overwhelming feeling that nothing she ever did would be good enough. Maybe you have had similar experiences.

As a husband who had never been through an experience like this, it was tough for me to watch. I wanted to step in and fix it, although there was nothing I would have been able to do. My wife struggled with it, and it caused her extreme stress.

However, Tabatha is a very motivated and driven woman, and she wouldn't wallow in the stress this situation was creating. She constantly sought wisdom and advice from others to help her through it. Little by little, she built up her education—formally through additional training and informally through mentorships. In turn, her capacity expanded until she was able to have peace around most of the experience.

But the story doesn't end there.

My Own Difficult Work Situation

Shortly after that, there was a leadership change in my work. I had gotten used to a father/son type relationship with my supervisor over several years. That was quickly yanked away from me. My new supervisor made it extremely clear that he was there to be my boss and that I'd "better not forget it."

I persevered through the next two years inside a pervasively declining culture. I was challenged to shield my team from the negative cultural effects and lead them to our own growth, in spite of the greater organizational decay.

The situation affected every aspect of my life for the entire duration of the experience. I was challenged *emotionally* as I tried to balance my true feelings with keeping a strong face for the team I was leading. I was challenged *spiritually* because I sought to love others and let the love of Jesus be evident through me. I had to *choose* love because I didn't feel it. I was challenged *financially* as the organizational culture made it difficult to perform at peak levels. I was challenged *personally* at home, with my family. I allowed my troubles at work to seep into my home life and infiltrate much of our conversation. At the time, I didn't like who I was becoming.

Thank God it wasn't up to me to decide if I would endure it, though! As it turns out, my wife's prior challenges in her role were a warmup of capacity building for what came later. I have enough material from these two years to write a future book, titled *Winning when You're Losing.* I will share with you a couple of capacity-building takeaways that will appear in the new book.

Two Valuable Lessons I Learned

John Maxwell's book *The 360 Degree Leader* was a game changer for me. It landed in my lap at the most opportune time. A main premise of the book is that leaders lead down, across, and up their organizations. Brilliant! My first epiphany came to me as a result of reading this book.

As a twenty-eight-year-old leader of one of the top teams inside a Fortune 100 company, I still had the responsibility of leading *up*. I had no positional authority, but that wasn't an excuse. I had to figure out a way, at a higher standard, to lead up. The removal of, and freedom from, helplessness that came from that notion was life changing. The capacity I developed because of the situation at work, combined with my comprehension of the concepts taught in Maxwell's book, was divine timing. Had I not been going through a "hard-knock" season, I would never have had the privilege of acquiring the newfound capacity.

The second invaluable lesson I learned from this arduous season was the value of enrollment. *Enrollment* is obtaining buy-in from key people inside your organization, particularly when the org-chart says you don't have to. This was a welcome revelation, a promising strategy I could try, when we experienced that leadership change and I was told what I was going to do and how I was going to do it, whether I liked it or not. I had felt like all my success and experience were for naught, but expanding my reach outside the org chart offered me new opportunities for a breakthrough.

At first, I viewed this strategy as the quickest way to drive a wedge inside our leadership team. I didn't see how it could help us reach our goal of building an organization that could help people in our community build their best lives. I couldn't understand why someone would make a leadership decision like that. It was against every book on leadership and any advice any coach had given me. I didn't understand—until I was in the same position.

Avoid the Temptation to Be a Dictator

Directly after those two years, I had the privilege of becoming a Managing Partner of an entire operation and inherited a team of my own. The team members, much like me, grew up professionally in that organization and had built a significant portion of it. I came into the picture, now thirty years old, *wise beyond my years*—or so I thought. I had grandiose visions for where we were headed. It was a race. We had to get to these visions as soon as possible. Or so I thought.

My first inclination was to dive headlong into *my* vision using *my* methods on *my* timeline. After all, I was the appointed leader. My innate desire to do this was extremely strong. In fact, it was so strong that the only way I would be able to overcome it was to experience firsthand the devastating effects of how wrong that strategy had been for a solid twenty-four months directly prior to my new role. I was doing the same thing my predecessors had.

In my prior situation, my ineffective boss had not enrolled any of his leadership team in his vision. He dictated what we would do—all the time. When I became a leader of an office, I was initially tempted to do the same thing because it seemed faster. Thankfully, I had seen the outcome of his approach to those prior twenty-four months, so I knew that the ultimate outcome wasn't faster, and it certainly wasn't ideal. So I slowed down and made sure I aligned my vision with that of everyone in that office before I charged forward.

I had to learn this through personal experience. I learned that a team is much more effective when the leader and the members work *together* toward solutions, benefiting from each individual's unique perspective and experience. When team members are part of the decision-making process, they are more committed to achieving a positive outcome.

The "hard-knock" capacity builder won again!

Learn to love the "hard knocks" you experience. Embrace them. Quantify the growth you gain from them. Look for opportunities to learn from them. This is how you experience winning when you're losing.

Athletics

For many of us, participation in athletics is a thing of the past, but I encourage you not to accept that as fate. There is so much good capacity-building education that can come from participating in athletics. Many people played on sports teams growing up. I want to take a forward-looking approach to how you can proactively incorporate athletics into your growth.

First, I want to address the belief some people have that those days are gone. A friend of mine, Mark Pfaff, sent me a book a couple years ago by Chris Crowley called *Younger Next Year: Live Strong, Fit, and Sexy: Until You're 80 and Beyond.*

The book contains a discussion by Crowley in which he recommends hiring a trainer to learn how to lift weights in a gym. He advises against trying to take shortcuts, such as buying gadgets or books that promise quick results without much work.

Crowley's personally convicting quote that really hit me says, "You're a grown-up, right? Then don't be a dope. The gadgets, or the weights, do not do the work. You do."[4]

If we want to live healthy, full lives that represent our best version of ourselves, then *we* must do the work. We have to exercise continually. For too many years, I thought my high-school varsity athletic letters were continuing to keep me healthy a decade later.

The fact that I "used to be able to (*fill in the blank*)" meant nothing to my current health.

Now, while this is not a book on living your best life through physical health, there is much to be gained through your education in the area of athletics.

In 2019, my family moved to the Minneapolis area. Tabatha and I have moved multiple times during our marriage. Each time, we find it as a good point in time to reinvent or re-present ourselves into a more modern version of who we want to become. In this latest move, I had decided that I was no longer going to ignore my need to exercise. The thought of hours of hamster-wheeling per week at 5:00 a.m. sounded like torture, and so I decided I was going to start playing basketball again.

So I found myself playing, five days a week. On Tuesdays, Thursdays, and Fridays, I got up at 4:45 a.m. to go play basketball for up to two hours at the local gym. On Saturday mornings, I played at a local church for about an hour. And on

---

4. Chris Crowley, *Younger Next Year: Live Strong, Fit, and Sexy: Until You're 80 and Beyond* (New York: Workman Publishing, 2019), 157.

Sunday nights, I played for ninety minutes at my daughters' school.

Giving myself about a ten-year break from basketball, developing my professional career, and then returning gave me a fresh perspective on all the things I could learn and apply to everyday life. For example, I had to rethink the adage that "it's all in your head." I have always read that whether you believe you can or you can't, you're right. Nothing has made this clearer than a good 5:00 a.m. basketball session. I could play my best game and still spend all morning on the loser's court.

It's all mental! What do you tell yourself about your shooting ability? How long do you dwell on the bad pass you just made? What is your internal dialogue about your shooting/passing ratio?

If you are confident in all your actions and maintain a "next" mindset, you are going to play like LeBron James. But if you second-guess yourself, get hung up on your mistakes, and feel self-conscious about your playing, not even Coach Wooden can help pull you out of the funk you are about to experience. This is true about the rest of our lives, too. The lessons we can learn from a game that we use to get exercise transitions completely to building our capacity in the rest of life.

My executive coach, Reed Moore, told me something several years ago that I will never forget. He was about to embark on a lifestyle change toward fitness, and he said, "Steve, how can I get up there and lead people at a high level when I am obviously fifty pounds overweight? No one is going to take anything I have to say seriously. So before I can become a next-level leader, I have to lead myself."

It stuck with me for years. Reed chose to start doing triathlons. If you know anything about triathlons, the training that's required is almost like a full-time job. Reed trained for hours for his bike rides, runs, and swims. Because of this extreme dedication, the community around triathlons is filled with an elite crew. As a newly inducted member into this tribe, Reed began to surround himself and build relationships (see Capacity Pillar number three) with people who helped him fast-forward his development toward building his best life. In turn, he began to excel as a coach and leader of teams, and countless others—including me—have benefited from his athletic endeavor and commitment.

My encouragement is this: if you haven't already, ignite your athletic journey. And if you have already, mine it for informal education, the mental challenges, the physical victories and defeats, and the mind game you learn as you compete with yourself and others. What you learn from this process will have positive implications in your sport of choice, as well as on your capacity ceiling!

Stress can often cause us to crumble, so use this as an opportunity to grow. Remember, whether you're dealing with financial setbacks, health problems, or workplace difficulties, if you increase your capacity ceiling, you'll be able to handle more.

Sometimes it's as easy as keeping problems in a proper perspective and adding meaning to negative experiences. It's also a matter of prioritizing what's important in your life. I believe we must take care of our physical health because the mind and body act as one. We can actually refuse to allow a pessimistic inner monologue to happen if we have a better relationship with our bodies, which we discover through these athletic adventures.

Family

You can choose your friends, but you can't choose your family. I am so thankful that God blessed me with a loving family. Much of my upbringing was *normal*, but that doesn't mean that there wasn't much to learn from my family.

My parents were amazing. My dad went to the United States Naval Academy and then worked in human resources for most of his career. My mom stayed home to raise my younger sister and me. They spent about 25 percent of their income to send my sister and me to the highest-rated, private Christian school in town.

This phenomenal sacrifice meant that there wasn't much money left over, but we had everything we needed. We had a comfortable, safe home in a nice neighborhood near our school and church. We had vehicles that ran most of the time. There just weren't a lot of extras. And thank goodness there weren't!

Because I received an early education about hard work from that upbringing, I had the privilege of having to figure out how to pay for all the extracurriculars I wanted to participate in. My first job was a learning lesson, which led me to start my first company at age fifteen.

My family also taught me the value and importance of budgeting. Because there weren't a lot of extras to go around, they allowed me to keep my permanent fund dividend (PFD). This was a check that the State of Alaska gave every resident each September. Yes, it is true, at least it was then, that you do get *paid* to live in Alaska. This typically amounted to $1,000. So, was it worth it to get *paid* to live in Alaska? You tell me!

The genius idea that my parents came up with was to give me this entire amount of money. In addition, I would get several hundred dollars from my grandparents for my birthday and Christmas. In exchange, I had to purchase everything. You name it—back-to-school supplies, clothes, hot lunches, sports team dues and equipment, road-trip costs, video games, and meals out with friends. Car modifications and repairs also came out of my own funds.

The value of being able to prepare a long-term forecast, budget, and then execute what I learned from this exercise was invaluable in my future endeavors. I also learned that money was not a finite or nonrenewable resource. This lesson started to craft the growth mindset that I have today. I knew that if I was running out of money, I had to go provide value for someone who was willing to exchange their money for what I could do to help them.

And that leads into one of the most formidable learning components in your informal education: starter jobs.

Starter Jobs

We all had them. Some of us had them earlier than others. Think back to yours. What was it? Burger flipping? Babysitting? Cutting the neighbor's lawn? Perhaps you worked maintenance at your school over the summer.

For many of us, this was a stressful time. We were maxing out our capacity ceiling on a daily basis. There were so many lessons to learn, habits to establish, and relationships to develop. That is why, for many of us, our starter job was so formidable.

I remember mine: commercial salmon fishing. Whoa! I was fourteen years old, ninety-eight pounds soaking wet, and in for a *big* surprise.

Let me introduce you to the schedule of a commercial salmon fisherman.

4:00 a.m.: You wriggle out of your sleeping bag, which is laid out on a plywood board on the ground, covered in sand because—let's face it—you are sleeping in a plywood shack on the beach. It is a crisp 41 degrees. Yet again, you choose to sleep in the clothes you fished in yesterday because when compared to slipping into your other sand-coated outfit, this just seems easier. You and your three roommates slide on your hip waders, still damp inside from yesterday's fishing. You clip on your life vest and then cover everything up with your heavy-duty commercial fishing rain gear. Grundens is what the pros typically use; however, my aforementioned budget precluded me from gearing up like the pros. So my rain gear was ripped and repaired almost daily with duct tape. Now you had your armor on.

5:00 a.m.: Time is passing quickly already, but you manage to walk the hundred yards to the skiffs, where you will spend the rest of the day fishing. You mow down a bowl potentially identifiable as oatmeal and drink two cans of Bluebird orange juice. Yuck! You will need every one of those calories, though, because you are about to expend them in the next sixty minutes.

Nets are nicely coiled in your 20-foot boat, and you hop in as the owner drives over in his 1950s *boom truck*. This is a custom fabricated truck that has what appears to be a unicorn tusk at the front, constructed of three three-inch steel pipes in a pyramid, welded together as they meet at the front tip. A large industrial carabiner dangles from a rusty steel cable that is attached to a winch that was manufactured well before my birth.

Inside the boat are three large straps that also clip together in the center and are attached to the carabiner (a metal ring with one spring-hinged side) from the boom truck. The winch strains as it lifts the boat up into the air. The truck drives us out into the ocean surf and lowers us down until the boat's buoyancy causes the cable to go slack. We start up the outboard motor, drop it into the saltwater, and unclip the straps from the carabiner.

5:05 a.m.: We arrive at our first net. It is my job to lean over the side of the boat, balancing at the waist and counteracting the rise and fall of the sea. At the precise moment we motor past the buoy, I am to grab it out of the ice-cold water and hoist it into the boat—on the first try. Time is money.

Fortunately, I got pretty good at this skill, so I typically was able to retrieve the buoy on the first attempt and rarely fell in the water doing so. (I did fall in one time).

After retrieving the buoy, we now have to clip the net that was neatly coiled in the boat to the buoy and toss it back in the ocean. Then we quickly motor to the coordinating buoy that is 50 yards away, bobbing in the ocean. If we coiled the net properly the prior evening, it will unfurl smoothly. However, if we were careless, due to the probably forty-eight-hour shift we had just pulled, occasionally there would be snags in the net.

What might happen next is the net will be quickly ejected into the ocean, and we will have to retrieve it without getting the spinning prop caught in the net. You can see the complications that could quickly arise in this routine task that was being carried out by boys who were just figuring out they needed to wear deodorant and who were green with envy as their fellow fifteen-year-old coworkers "needed" to shave in the mornings.

Upon dispensing all the net and reaching the coordinating buoy, I once again hoist myself over the railing of the boat and deftly retrieve the large orange ball. I finish the set by clipping the other end of the net to the correct buoy and toss it overboard, Now we were fishing! Only five more sets to go!

6:00 a.m.–6:00 p.m.: After about an hour, we have the entire infrastructure established for a whole day of fishing. We circle back to the first net we set that has been wet (in the water) the longest. The captain motors us up to the now-very-taught corkline that runs between the two buoys and floats on top of the water. I now perform my acrobatic act again, this time leaning over the very tip of the bow of the boat. Upon contact with the corkline, I grasp it underhand with both hands and then shift my weight back toward the inside of the boat. As the corkline lays across the bow, I quickly lean back onto it so that it won't escape back into the frigid water. Then, hand over hand, I pull the rest of the net over the bow until I get to the lead line that is weighted about eight feet into the water.

We then slide the entire net, stretched out over the length of the boat, and pull ourselves along the fifty yards of it, dropping salmon onto the floor of the boat as they jump over the side rail. This pattern continue net to net until we have several thousand pounds of salmon flopping around in the hull of our boat.

Once we start to sit low in the water due to the newly acquired cargo, we drive up to a large tender boat. Their crew maneuvers the crane over our small skiff, and we hand-toss all the salmon into the giant net. Then we're off to load up with more fish.

This pattern continues all day long.

6:00 p.m.: After devouring our dinner, we take a few minutes to debrief with the crews from the other boats about the day, and then head straight back out to work. We load up our boat, net by net, until we need to offload at the tender and then start again.

Most of the time, the openers, when we could fish, were forty-eight to ninety-six hours long. This meant we would fish nearly the entire time. At about 10:00 p.m., we would do one final round, load up from the six nets, and then beach our boats. We would take a two-hour nap in our sand-coated sleeping bags, let the nets soak, and then wake up to do another round of harvesting. This rotation would continue throughout the entire opener.

This pattern continued throughout my four weeks of commercial fishing. As an independent contractor, I was not guaranteed anything. A month or so after the end of the season, I would get a check from the owner based on the total amount of fish caught and my share. After all was said and done, I believe my net take-home pay was somewhere around $4.00 per hour, but I was happy. I was able to purchase my first snowmobile and put some cash in the bank to help bolster my budget for the upcoming school year.

Two Important Outcomes of My Starter Job

I learned so much in those four weeks of commercial fishing that I could not have been taught as effectively any other way. Here are the two main takeaways that were engrained in my DNA for the rest of my life:

1. The value of hard work

Compared to what I had accomplished as a fourteen-year-old, ninety-eight-pound boy, nothing would ever be harder!

I also learned that much of the physical work we do is also mental. My body and mind could accomplish things that most people considered impossible, yet these fishermen lived it, day in and day out. This set the foundation for me to be able to accomplish multiples of what my peers could, throughout my career.

Most of us believe we are hard workers. We went to college. We got good grades. We got jobs. We did exactly what our fathers and high school guidance counselors told us to do. We get out of bed, we go to work, and we pay our bills. We keep ourselves and our homes neat and tidy, and we go to bed each night feeling somewhat exhausted.

But the problem with that conception of hard work is that it's not what all those successful people meant when they gave you the advice to "work hard, and you can achieve anything."

Most of what we do on a day-to-day basis is simply what we have to do to survive. Your job, your chores, your obligations to your family, and the favors to your friends—that's not hard work. That's regular work. That's your routine—the stuff that you and every other human being do every single day.

Hard work is what you do *on top of* all that. It's what you do after you've put in your eight hours, after you've cleaned your apartment, after you've kept all your appointments and followed through on all your promises. Hard work is above and beyond—and at times, it's the only thing that will push *your capacity* above and beyond.

Earlier, I mentioned that doing more doesn't mean working more hours. There are, however, seasons that will require more hours. These seasons typically have defined beginning and end dates, with specific objectives. The hard work that goes into these seasons can be powerful education sessions that teach you how to accomplish just as much without having to put that many hours in perpetually.

2. Entrepreneurship skills

During my starter job, I learned something important about myself: I didn't enjoy having a boss. The man who owned the camp was very wise, structured, disciplined, and difficult to work for—but fair. I could do the math, and I knew how much was made during that short time. I also knew how much we could have made, more or less. I learned that to accomplish what I wanted to in life, I would have to bet on myself by working for myself, not for someone else.

These lessons have stuck with me and have weaved their way throughout my life. They are lessons that no formal education could have embedded in me.. Although they were some of the hardest days of my life, commercial fishing built the foundation of what would become the trajectory of my working career.

Books

If you have made it this far in the book, chances are, you are a reader. If you are like me, though, that hasn't always been the case.

Many of us learned how to read in kindergarten. I never went to kindergarten (well, I did for three weeks, and then we moved, and I never reenrolled).

When I was about to start first grade, my mom said to my dad, "I think Steven needs to know how to read to go into first grade. Can you teach him?"

So my dad sat me down with a book and asked me to read it to him. I did. My Grandma June would read to us a lot. A few minutes later, my dad called out to my mom, "He's good. He knows how."

Initially, I couldn't get enough. I read all the time. Our first-grade teacher created a contest for the most books read, and I would gobble them up so fast that she would make me reread them because she didn't believe I could possibly have read them that quickly. My appetite for reading grew and grew.

Do you remember reading those books produced by a company called *The Great Illustrated Classics*? They were popular in the 1990s and offered a great way for young readers to read through many classic literary stories. I loved them. They were 300 pages, but every other page was a picture. The stories were amazing. They were classics, after all. It allowed me to connect with my dad, uncle, and granddad because these were the same books they read growing up. I remember getting in trouble at night because I would read an entire book after going to bed at night.

And then at some point, that stopped. I believe it was after moving to Alaska when I was in the fourth grade. It was no longer cool to read. I was doing everything in my power to fit in and make new friends, and I found out that reading wasn't cool to them. Therefore, in the interest of wanting to fit in, I curtailed my voracious reading habits. As an aside, this is an example of where the wrong *relationships* can be counteractive to building your capacity.

Disclaimer: If you were one of my English teachers when I was growing up, you might want to skip the next section (sorry, Mrs. Edwards). From about fifth grade, all the way through college, I never read a book. I utilized all kinds of shortcuts—CliffsNotes, summaries, first pages of each chapter. You name it, I tried it. I was able to get through the rest of my formal education without reading the books I was assigned. I even wore this as a badge of honor for many years (much to the chagrin of my lovely wife, Tabatha).

Until a few years ago.

I was in the middle of leading my first office as the Managing Partner, and I decided it was time to hire a professional coach. This was a no-brainer for me because I have always looked up to, and wanted to emulate all aspects of, the life of a man named Reed Moore. He had just started to offer professional coaching services to a limited clientele.

We began in December, so naturally, the conversation of goals for the upcoming year surfaced. Reed asked how many books I planned to read in the next year. The good news is, I knew that question was coming. As I prepared to engage in our coaching relationship, I started researching, and I began to come to grips with the mantra that "leaders are readers."

So I proudly echoed back, "I will commit to reading one book a month next year!"

The consummate professional, Reed refrained from laughing. He kindly said, "Steve, that's great, but most people in your position of leadership read about one book a week. Why don't we meet in the middle and have you start out with two books a month?"

I hesitated but said, "OK, deal."

Not knowing how I was going to do it, I followed his guidance on book titles. Nearly all were self-development nonfiction books. Later, I would become comfortable exploring my own titles.

I quickly became the "I just got done reading...you have to read it!" guy at parties and work conferences. It was amazing.

I finished the year at nearly forty books read and haven't looked back since! Here are a few ground rules that I have followed that have empowered me to consume the best content and a rapid pace.

1.   **You don't have to finish the book.** This realization was empowering to me. Most authors put their best content in the beginning of the book and then spend the rest of the book elaborating. You might even accuse me of doing this. If you are not drawn in or impressed by the first 20 percent of the book, you probably aren't going to get much more in the back 80 percent. And even if you do, typically, the best stuff is up front. I probably finish 80 percent of the books I start reading, but almost all are strong recommendations from people I trust. That said, I still terminate my relationship with about 20 percent of books because early chapters do not draw me in.

2.   **Audiobooks are your friend.** Audible.com is one of the most powerful tools I have used in my career. Work your way

up to listening to the content at two times the normal speed—or more, if you can handle it. This means you can finish an eight-hour book in four hours.

According to the US Census Bureau, the average American's commute grew to just over twenty-seven minutes one way in 2018, a record high. The average American has added about two minutes to their one-way commute since 2009.[5]

Of course the COVID-19 pandemic changed all that, as millions of people worked from home. But if you are one of those people who will return to an office, you can decide to turn off talk radio or music and listen to audiobooks instead. By making that one change, your commute can turn into a CEO leadership workshop, and you can go through one book per week.

Listening to audiobooks is the key to the leadership skills I have developed over the past years, and it was the impetus for me to write this book. Listening is learning, just as reading is learning.

3. **Keep score.** Whether you use a tool like goodreads.com or just a notes app on your phone, write down the title of every book you read. Every time someone recommends a book to you, add it to your list of books to read. Note who recommended it to you and why.

---

5. "Nine Days on the Road. Average Commute Time Reached a New Record Last Year," Christopher Ingraham, *The Washington Post*, October 7, 2019, https://www.washingtonpost.com/business/2019/10/07/nine-days-road-average-commute-time-reached-new-record-last-year/.

This does a couple things. It constantly gives you fresh content to read, and it gives you an opportunity to follow up with the person once you finish the book. This will allow you to build credibility with this person, further enhancing your relationship with him or her. If you are a competitive person like me, you are motivated by seeing your "score" improve over time.

I have found the most effective model to really make what you read stick is as follows: read, take notes, apply, teach.

To increase my capacity and really make my reading education stick, I have found it is important to *teach* what I am reading. I try to do this on a weekly basis through a couple forums I have created inside my organization. I have found that you create a cadence of accountability for yourself when you do this because no one wants to be a hypocrite. If you teach others what you have learned, then you are probably going to follow your own advice. You don't want others to catch you saying one thing but doing another.

Book Clubs

I also recently started a monthly book club inside my organization. Here are a few of the reasons for doing this.

First, I wanted to reread some of the more impactful books that I had consumed early in my reading journey. There are seasons of quantity and seasons of quality. After consuming a large quantity of books the past couple of years, my focus this year is on quality. I am in a substantially different season of life now and can unearth some new nuggets from the previous treasures I discovered. I started the book club to implant accountability into this goal. I have created a venue in which I am forced to report on the in-depth findings of the books I have reread.

I also realized there is a certain beauty and unity that result when the people you surround yourself with are all learning the same things from the same books. Unity within our organization speeds up, and so does trust. You gain the advantage of other perspectives on the same content to maximize the experience. Communing as a group and debriefing one another on the content allows us to garner the maximum amount of value from books I have pre-vetted and found to have a high impact.

The purpose of any club is to bring a community together and discuss something that matters to them. Our book club is absolutely no different.

In my humble opinion, reading books is the top thing you can do to supercharge growth, handle stress, and live your best life!

Coaching

Many of us had coaches all through our lives as we grew up. They were influential in molding who we became. Whether it was the coach for our fourth-grade basketball team, our junior high cross-country coach, or high school football, or if it was our band director, we all learned from someone who was more experienced than us and was a subject-matter expert in whatever area we were engaging in.

This person could see things that were in our blind spots. They helped us become better versions of ourselves than sometimes we ever even thought possible. They studied our actions and movements long after they occurred. They took it upon themselves to guide us into an even better outcome.

They taught us how to have fun and how to compete. They taught us the ground rules for interpersonal relationships in a competitive environment. They celebrated some of life's most sweet victories. They were there to provide a shoulder to cry on when we suffered some of life's greatest defeats. Looking back, many of us would have a difficult time naming a more influential relationship in our formidable years than a coach.

Yet, for some reason, when we grow up and become adults, we forget about these integral relationships we had in our lives. We trade those volunteer leaders for tenured professors and washed-up managers. We're disappointed when they don't provide us the feedback or guidance we so desperately need as we try to grow our capacity for stress. It seems as if we are the only ones who care about our personal development. And for the most part, we're right.

Enter hiring a professional business coach.

My first recollection of the existence of business coaches was listening to my boss recount his latest session with his professional coach. Quite frankly, I don't even recall what he said. I was too distracted when I learned that he had paid $250 for the thirty-minute session. To my new-to-leadership ears, I couldn't possibly fathom how any conversation could be worth that amount of money. From that point forward, I had to figure out why people smarter, wiser, and more experienced than me had no problem paying business coaches.

This is where my coaching relationship with Reed began. He reached out to me to let me know he had a spot for me if I wanted it. At the time, I wasn't quite ready for it, but I asked him to let me know when his last spot was about to be taken. Then I went to work thinking about how I could afford to pay his monthly coaching fee.

The problem was, I was asking the wrong question. I needed to be asking myself, "What value do I need to get from coaching so that the monetary cost is a no-brainer?"

Once I concluded that I was going to hire a coach, I wanted to make sure I was very clear that Reed was going to be able to speak truth, encouragement, and direction into my life.

I knew Reed was the coach for me. But because I was going to be investing a lot of time and money in this business relationship, I wanted to be 100 percent sure I was hiring the right person. So I decided to do an objective assessment of what I needed to get out of the relationship. Here are four considerations I looked at when deciding whom to hire as my coach:

1. **My coach needed to be personally more successful in business than I had been.** I needed to trust his or her firsthand experience on getting me to where I wanted to go and had to do it by leading through other people versus being a sole proprietor or a one-person show. This was the method I wanted to use to grow my business. The coach also had to be practicing in business

versus having experience only in professional coaching. I wanted to be able to trust that his or her experience and advice were imminently relevant.

2. **It was also important to me that the coach did not function under a workaholic mentality.** I wanted to work with someone who had a great grasp on living an integrated and balanced lifestyle successfully.

3. **The coach needed to have a model relationship with his or her spouse and be a fantastic parent.** I believe that if someone has all the professional success in the world but fails as a spouse and parent, it's all for nothing. I wanted my coach to have personal evidence for a successful model in this area of life.

4. **My coach had to have an evangelical Christian life view.** This is important to me because I frame my decisions in business and in life based on the teachings of Jesus Christ in the Bible. I didn't want to have to translate anything my coach said into my own worldview. The purer the content, the more quickly I could put it into practice.

It was no small task to find someone who lived up to the sum of all these requirements. Very few people I have ever met would be able to meet all those criteria, let alone professionally coach other leaders. Not to mention willing to work with a young twenty-something new leader.

But Reed clearly met all my criteria.

I felt very blessed to have a relationship with this man and be able to hire him as my professional coach. I was certain I would not be able to find someone else who met my criteria.

One of the biggest things I was able to garner from my coaching sessions was a substantially improved capacity. In fact, many of the principles in the Capacity Model are life lessons stemming from my coaching conversations.

I fully believe that to have an optimal relationship with your coach, they cannot also be your manager. I have had great leaders as my bosses for much of my career. But at the end of the day, your relationship with your boss cannot be a pure coaching relationship. They need you to perform in your role. And if you don't perform, your job is on the line. When they ask you questions, you can't help but be at least slightly politically correct in your answers. No matter how good your relationship is.

I believe a great manager can provide an incredible amount of guidance and accountability to get you to your peak performance level. A coach also can help you think through systems and models as you begin to build your leadership style in the brand you represent with your people. Coaches also can give you the confidence to have the tough conversations, make the difficult decisions that will make or break your career, change your marriage, and enhance all other lifelong relationships.

There have been many times when I reached out to my coach to ask him to give me a pep talk on a conversation I already knew needed to happen with someone. These tipping-point conver-sations have been defining moments in my past. I know that without my coach, I would not have stepped up to the plate in many of those scenarios.

I would be remiss if I didn't mention that my income has gone up over 100 percent the past few years since I hired my coach. Together, we have found a way for him to pay for himself: win–win.

Seminars and Workshops

It is interesting to me how many of us spend the first eighteen years of our lives participating in group learning sessions, more commonly known as school. However, once we advanced into our *adult* years, we completely abandon this form of learning in our lives. But they present great opportunities to continue your growth and learning. Professional seminars and workshops can be some of the most transformative and capacity-building events in which we can invest our time and money.

Many of us have witnessed the advertisements and social media posts for the self-help gurus and professional speakers who put on these seminars and workshops. They seem to emerge from the woodwork; there are so many of them. However, I believe that the fact that the industry has been around for centuries lends proof to the impact that they have on people's lives.

I have been fortunate that in my career, my company has sponsored most of these events for me. Typically, the sessions I like to attend are arranged around success, how to get to the next level, or how to win in my professional world. However, I have found that the most impactful time I spend is socializing with the other people who have taken time from their busy schedules to attend these events. I learn from them. I find that this *informal* type of learning allows me to craft the areas that I will learn more about.

This is done by asking questions of my peers who are in a very similar stage of life as me, and listening to their experiences and their answers. It also allows me to consider the source whenever I'm having these conversations because I know my peers and what many of their strengths and weaknesses are. It is truly a blessing that I've been able to attend seminars and workshops with some frequency. I'm very thankful to my company as well as my colleagues who have all chosen to invest in this amazing capacity building informal education.

Podcasts

Finally, I want to discuss probably the most contemporary type of informal but effective education—the podcast.

While the ability for people to disseminate information over the audio airwaves has existed for many decades, the ability to access it at the tip of our fingers and filter it down to the most minute, specific categories is a relatively recent invention. What is so incredible about podcasts is that on demand, you can access any topic on which you want to increase your capacity and get high-caliber, on-point information that's extremely relevant to your world in a twenty-minute snippet.

This is in direct contrast to the audiobook, which may take four to eight hours to consume the information. A podcast breaks content into digestible, conversational chunks. This allows you to curate a library of podcasters who align with your worldview and values. They begin to add new learning into your world, twenty to thirty minutes at a time.

My wife, who is a professional life coach, is a voracious consumer of podcasts. Podcasts feed her desire to grow her capacity in specific areas. They have provided the greatest source of knowledge, learning, and forward-thinking, relevant development for her business. She has been able to find coaches, mentors, and vendors to help move her business forward through the world of podcasts. I can honestly say her business would have struggled significantly to get off the ground without the incorporation of regular podcast listening.

Part 3: Habits

I really, truly felt like I didn't belong. I sat there and listened to a man I deeply respected and considered one of the most disciplined people I know. Yet I couldn't believe the conversation I was hearing.

"One hundred twenty miles? I might just go halfway with you and then turn around," my coach, Reed, commented.

"Come on! Are you really that out of shape?" Adam taunted.

"I haven't been training for a while, so you're going to have to do the last sixty without me."

Reed and Adam had spent the previous ten minutes going back and forth, talking nonchalantly about twenty-mile runs and hundred-mile bike rides as if they were warmups for a main event.

I've always been an athletic guy, but what they were doing was more on the level of superhuman. I quietly listened and offered no input or feedback because I legitimately had none.

Welcome to the triathlete subculture.

This was certainly a place I knew I didn't belong. I now had gained an entirely new level of perspective on what it meant to be in shape. And more pertinent to the matter at hand, I learned what it meant to be disciplined to the max.

I'm sure you have somebody in your life whom you look up to as the definition of *discipline*, or self-control.

Sometimes, these are the people who get up at 4:30 a.m. seven days a week to do their prayer, affirmations, reading, stretching, yoga, running, biking, racquetball, meal prep, calling their parents or grandparents, reading to their kids, washing their cars, and mowing their lawns—all before they eat breakfast. We look at people like that and think, "I wish I were that disciplined!"

There's a beautiful truth to discipline, though. It's not a mythical attainment that is reserved for a select few elite human beings. No, discipline is merely a collection of intentional habits. This superhuman friend whom you are graced to be in a relationship with was not born into some disciplined birthright. He or she has done the hard, boring, monotonous work of building a collection of small habits over a long period of time, and now the sum of their parts creates a perception of heroic discipline.

A *habit* is defined as a regular tendency or practice that is hard to give up. When we properly coordinate these tendencies in alignment with our goals and aspirations and follow up with vigor, we can significantly increase our capacity ceiling.

As we take a deeper dive into the habits we can establish to help us build our capacity, it's important to understand what the three different types of habits are: *being*, *relating*, and *doing*.

Everything good comes in threes.

Chapter 8: "Being" Habits

"Being" habits are habits that we establish to better ourselves. Many of these habits are ones you've probably tried to establish in the past, not knowing that they, in turn, were also there to build your capacity.

When it comes to building habits, I think it's helpful to throw all your ideas together and then see how they interact with each other. Identify the crossover and potential conflicts, as well as identifying synergies that will help build extra momentum in implanting the habit into the regular cadence of your life.

Just as there are three types of habits (*being*, *relating*, and *doing*) that you can build, each of these has—you guessed it— three components. In building our "being" habits, we will look at *physical*, *spiritual*, and *intellectual* habit categories. I will explain and give examples of each one so you can draw out the application for your own life and develop a well-rounded strategy to build out this area of your capacity. Each person's capacity-building journey will be different, and that's OK!

Let's look at the three components of "being" habits.

1. Physical Habits

Each of us gets only one body, one chance to do it right.

The Bible refers to our bodies as temples. Solomon's temple in the Old Testament is one of the most famous in history. Upon completion, it was one of the most ornate and expensive buildings in ancient days. It was wrought in precious metals, meticulously crafted by the hands of some of the most skilled artisans of the time. Workers labored to build it, day in and day out, for seven years. It wasn't just the eighty-four months constructing the temple that was astounding, but also the decades leading up to it during which the artisans were perfecting their craft.

The analogy of the human body being a temple can be helpful to us. We can draw on what we know of what it takes to construct a temple, and that gives us insight into the extent to which we could establish positive physical habits in our lives.

I am certainly not advocating that we forsake all else and spend seven years sculpting our physical bodies. I am saying that the habits we establish around our bodies manifest themselves into other areas of our capacity.

There are two areas in which we can establish habits to develop our physical being: exercise and diet.

A. Exercise

A favorite book of mine is *The Primal Blueprint* by Mark Sisson. It has done much to shape my perspective on the importance of exercise. While there are many people in our world who take exercise to the extreme, it is important that *all* of us take exercise to at least a minimum level.

The premise of the book is that our primal ancestors did not die from the same ailments that kill us today—at least not in the same way. Granted, their life spans were shorter because now we have modern-day medicine, but heart disease, high cholesterol, diabetes, cancer, and many other modern diseases are brought on by a sedentary lifestyle—our kryptonite.

Our ancestors had to walk to get anywhere, resulting in many minutes or hours a day of low-impact exercise. To replicate their exercise habit, I now take a thirty- to forty-five-minute walk four or five times a week. This is something nearly anybody can do! And it can be the difference between life and death.

This cadence of the rest of your life can certainly sustain a healthy lifestyle. Balanced with the right diet, there are obviously multiple levels beyond this that you can go. For me, endless hours on the treadmill, stationary bike, or elliptical just wasn't an option. I had to find something social and competitive to do.

I was in the best physical shape of my life when I was playing college basketball while also participating in intramural sports and being on the track team. To think of doing that now doesn't compute in my brain.

Back then, it was my job, although it didn't really feel like a job. And that was the point. I truly loved every second of it! Maybe not running "sweet-sixteens" until I puked, but *almost* every second of it!

Although I couldn't join a college basketball team at thirty-three years of age, I could find a group of guys who had all lived that life a decade or two prior. Thankfully, I was able to find this group within just a couple weeks of arriving in Minnesota. One of the things I love about this group is that it's a high-caliber, disciplined group of men.

Now that I have been with this group for more than a year and gotten to know them, it's no surprise that these are some of the leading professionals and business owners in town. Disciplined people have established a set of habits and conduct them regularly. Successful people surround themselves with successful people, and taking care of your physical health by exercising is one of the best things you can do to put yourself on the right path for increasing your capacity.

B. Diet

One of the statements someone made to me as I began the journey of establishing solid physical habits was, "You can't outwork the fork."

The point here is that no matter how much you exercise, in a matter of minutes, you can consume more calories than you burned off, negating all the effort you just painstakingly exerted.

For whatever reason, those simple five words have stuck with me ever since: "You can't outwork the fork." I've tried many diets and meal plans and made many resolutions. Some of them have worked well, particularly the keto diet. It was through four months of rigorous habits in sticking to the keto diet that I was able to prove to myself that I could lose some of the fifty excess pounds I had acquired in my adult life. I was able to drop roughly half of them over those four months.

And while I did gain some of them back after curtailing the diet, this confidence I gained, realizing that I am in control of my physical destiny, set me on a path to create new and better habits.

STRATEGIES THAT HELP ME CONTROL MY CALORIC INTAKE

Now, out of the fear and hope that someday we get to meet in person, I must confess that this is not something I have fully conquered, by any means. My habits around my diet are an ever-evolving battle. I would like to share with you a few things that I have found to be effective in capacity building around the food I put into my body.

Every friendship, including the one with your body, requires attention, care, and time. And quality of time is critical. It might take a while before you learn to be emotionally invested in your body. It will also take time for this friendship to bear ripe fruit—similar to your eating habits. In this transition phase, you should be positive and supportive of your own efforts.

I eat only when I'm hungry

First, and this might seem ridiculously simple, I try to eat only when I'm hungry. At first glance, you might think this is a day-by-day game-time decision. For many years, for me, it was. That's why I failed. When I say "I eat only when I'm hungry," I mean that I am consistently hungry only during certain parts of each day. I rarely feel hungry in the morning.

Besides all the benefits of intermittent fasting that we can achieve by not eating from dinner the night before until lunch the next day, I give myself less opportunity to screw up and overeat if I tell myself, "You're not hungry. So don't start eating."

I avoid binge-eating at lunch

Also, I am careful not to binge eat when I have lunch. This is where years of failing has led me to what works. I work in a business where it is extremely appropriate and profitable to have *business lunches* five days a week. The problem with business lunches is that they're held at a restaurant where I am continuously upsold on consuming more food than I need when I haven't eaten in the past sixteen hours. You can see the potential for failure here.

So instead, I have forgone nearly all business lunches and shifted to coffee meetings. (I love a good, nitro cold brew from Starbucks, and it has fewer calories than other options). I stock up on high-quality frozen paleo meals that are pre-portioned to contain between 300 and 400 calories. I eat one of those (or two, if I'm extremely hungry) and still consume 50 to 100 percent fewer calories than I would if I went out to that Italian restaurant for the fourth time this week.

I keep no snack foods at work

I don't keep any snacks at the office, so this leaves only dinner as the remaining variable in my caloric consumption for the day. Candidly, based on the types of food that my wife fills our refrigerator with, I can try my hardest to go off the rails and still win for the day because of all the guardrails I have put around the other twenty-three hours of my day. I have found this to be the most practical and effective strategy for instilling good diet habits and, in turn, avoiding derailing all the physical habits I have put in place.

2. Spiritual Habits

I think it's important for me to start off this section on spiritual habits by stating that I subscribe to an evangelical Judeo-Christian view of God. I was raised in a Christian household, attending Baptist and nondenominational Christian churches. I went through a private Christian education from kindergarten all the way through high school. I even attended a private Christian university during my freshman year of college. It is impossible for me to separate my view on growing capacity through spiritual habits from my own worldview.

My relationship with God encourages me to love and respect all of humankind because we all were created in God's image.

I believe there are two sets of habits that have been instrumental in my spiritual growth. They help me grow my relationship with my God by talking to Him and by learning about Him. I break these into two categories: reading the Bible and praying.

A. READING THE BIBLE

Similar to other reading habits, there are multiple approaches to consuming the Word of God. I believe the most important one is that I do it regularly—daily, if possible.

However, I have found that there are different seasons in life that require different cadences and approaches to reading the Bible. Here are different methods I have used and found to be effective, as well as a bonus approach.

Reading through the Bible in a year

Maybe you have heard of this and signed up for a reading plan or even bought a Bible that was divided neatly into 365 sections so you could conveniently pace yourself through this goal.

When I reflect on how aspirational this used to seem to me, I cringe slightly. The reason is, if I truly profess faith in God and want His help with everything I do, how could I possibly do that if I haven't consumed all the wisdom He has shared with us?

While I have accomplished this feat multiple times now, it amazes me that nearly every day, I uncover a new truth seemingly hidden in God's Word. It truly is a living, breathing manuscript that is meant to encourage and guide us in our everyday lives.

As with all habits, I have found that putting a system in place to create structure around it is the best way to ensure it gets accomplished. There are many apps you can download on your phone that will allow you to customize your plan to ensure that you read through the Bible in a specific amount of time. Make sure that you turn on the notifications so you are reminded constantly to read a segment, in case you forget to do so.

You can also purchase an audiobook version of the Bible, which will allow you to increase the listening speed and consume more content at a time. Although this isn't a great option for in-depth study, it is a great strategy for making your way through the entire Bible more quickly.

The Sprint

This was a new concept for me that our church recently did as a congregation for the month of January. We divided the entire New Testament into thirty daily reading sections. This worked out to about forty-five minutes a day of reading. At the end, we had collectively read through the entire New Testament.

I loved this approach because it allowed our congregation to connect over the same readings each day. We consumed the entire story of Jesus and the early church over and over again. I highly recommend doing this type of reading plan at least once a year.

The SOAP

SOAP stands for Scripture, Observation, Application, and Prayer. The idea is that you read a predetermined passage of Scripture each day with a group of people, write down your observations from the passage, and then write out how you plan to apply those concepts in your own life. At the end of each session, you pray through these takeaways.

I typically don't follow the journaling portion of this. This is an area of my life in which I have an opportunity to grow my capacity. What I do enjoy is the regular cadence of reading Scripture, combined with my community reading the same things. You have probably noticed that in each of these approaches, there is a component of community. I believe this accountability and group activity allows a more authentic and deep relationship to develop with those who are a part of it when we come together.

If you do not have a group to study with, you can download our church's app (River Valley Church, at

https://www.rivervalley.org/) and follow along with the SOAP section that is updated each day. Also, many virtual communities are available in various Bible apps.

A Proverb a Day

Another activity I like to do is to read a chapter of Proverbs each day. Solomon is one of the wisest men to have ever lived, and we have been gifted with thirty-one chapters of his greatest insights. One of the most powerful things we can ask God for is wisdom. I believe that the words recorded in Proverbs are one of the biggest gifts He has ever given to us.

Similar to the other approaches, I feel this is best done in a group as well. I have collaborated with many other highly successful businessmen using this method as a group, working individually.

Each morning, on our own time, we read the corresponding chapter to which day of the month it is. For example, on September 5th, we would read Proverbs Chapter 5. We then would write down our takeaways from the passage in the group text. This supercharged my growth and forced me to express articulately what I was going to implement based on what I had just read. It also prompted me to review the perspectives on the same material from other very talented people.

More community-based habits, for the win!

B. PRAYER

My prayer time has encompassed some of the most important experiences in my life. It has also been the most sporadic. I feel it is incredibly important to pray constantly.

In fact, the Bible exhorts us to "pray without ceasing" (see 1 Thessalonians 5:17, KJV).

Prayer is a way to build your relationship with God. Think about it. How do you build a relationship with someone else? You spend time with them—talking, telling stories, asking questions, learning. You can do all these are things in prayer.

My personal prayer patterns have followed a couple different of thought processes.

Keep a List

I keep a running list of all the people and things I am praying for in a notes file on my phone. Each time I pray, which is usually right after I finish reading my Bible passage for the day, I review this list.

There are typical items on there like my family, my job, etc. My favorite thing to do is to think about people in my world who are in need and then pray for them regularly. The reward comes when I see them next. Often, these are people I see only once a year.

It is such a powerful experience to see them; ask how they are doing, particularly in the area in which I have been praying for them; and then let them know I have been praying for them every day for the past year. You can only imagine the gratitude and thanks that wash across their faces.

An incredible former pastor of mine, Tommy Politz, of Hillside Christian Church in Amarillo, Texas, preached an incredible sermon one time about the wisdom that God gives us if we only ask. He recounted the sheer volume, complexity, and importance of the daily decisions he makes. He challenged us, as leaders, to beg for wisdom every day from the Lord.

James 1:5 says, "If any of you lacks wisdom, you should ask God, who gives generously to all without finding fault, and it will be given to you" (NIV).[6]

I hang the outcome of every day on this promise. What is at stake each day is the mission God has given me of helping others build their best lives. Why wouldn't I ask the omniscient creator of the universe for His wisdom in working through me each day?!

Pray with Your Spouse

Another important area of prayer is with your spouse. Early in marriage, someone advised me to begin every day in prayer with my wife. For years, we followed this advice. We were able to pray about many things together and see God answer— sometimes affirmatively and sometimes not, but always in our

---

6. Scripture taken from the Holy Bible, New International Version®, NIV®. Copyright © 1973, 1978, 1984, 2011 by Biblica, Inc.™ Used by permission of Zondervan. All rights reserved worldwide (www.zondervan.com). The "NIV" and "New International Version" are trademarks registered in the United States Patent and Trademark Office by Biblica, Inc.™

best interest. These outcomes were always encouraging. This is a great way to develop your relational capacity with your spouse.

We typically prayed together on the edge of our bed as I would leave early in the morning for the gym or office. Sadly, though, this many-year habit has fallen to the wayside through the stay-at-home orders associated with the COVID-19 environment.

During the pandemic, I watched Tabatha get up earlier to start her morning off as she spends the daytime growing her business, while I took advantage of a slower pace and delayed my wakeup time. This eroded our habit and, in effect, has removed a very precious time in our lives. I look forward to reestablishing this habit today! It truly is a crucial component of Tabatha and my best life.

Chapter 9: "Relating" Habits

The next type of habits is "relating" habits. There is some overlap between this discussion and the "Relationship" section. But here, I will discuss habits around important relationships and describe how to build capacity by growing through habits inside those relationships.

While there are many relationships that matter, I feel like the most effective ones to build habits around to grow your capacity are your marital, parental, and social relationships. Let's take a deeper dive into each of these.

1. Marital Habits

Out of our marital habits flows a high degree of our success in building our lives. The phrase "happy wife, happy life"—although not the most intellectually stimulating quote—certainly has merit.

I know my wife is happiest when she feels connected to me. So most of the habits I embrace center around creating environments for us to connect. Marital habits create a stronger connection, which, in turn, creates more trust. This trust increases our capacity to handle more stress together as a couple because we view each other as members of the same team.

My favorite forums for connecting with my wife are regular date nights, going to professional counseling together, and taking family road trips. I want to share some details about each one of these.

A. Date Night

This one seems like a no-brainer. However, if I asked you when your last scheduled date night was, what would you say? Ours was two weeks ago. We sat on the back porch, on purpose, put our phones away, and just talked. What made it a date was that it was planned. We made each other a priority.

During different seasons of my life, I have scheduled date nights at a regular time and then assigned my assistant to give me suggestions for each date night. I would then have her make the reservations and send calendar invites to my wife with details. As cold and corporate as this sounds, we had our most success in conducting regular dates during that season. The key is to talk to your spouse, tell him or her what you plan to do, and *why* you are doing it to get buy-in. Then execute.

During your date, the talking part is where the magic comes in. This can make or break the date. How many subjects do you switch between? How deep does the conversation go before you change subjects? A best-practice habit here is to try to go three levels deep. Here's an example of what that might look like, with me beginning a conversation with Tabatha. In this conversation, we actually went to four levels:

LEVEL 1:

"Honey, what were you most excited about at work this past week?"

"Well, I got to finish my new Facebook live interview with Amanda."

LEVEL 2:

"I saw that. Great job! I really liked how you dug into why she does her diet consulting. I feel like she really does have a passion for that. How did that make you feel about your passion for life coaching others?"

"You know, it certainly reminded me that it's important to keep that at the forefront of my mind. I feel like I can sometimes get so lost in the mundane day-to-day administrative tasks of running my business that, at times, I lose vision for my purpose of changing women's lives. But Amanda's passion was a great reminder for me to identify that regularly."

LEVEL 3:

"Wow, I can see how that can be infectious. Have you given more thought about how to communicate that?"

"A little bit. I brought it up with my coach, Sam today. She helped me come up with a list of priorities I want to communicate pertaining to my mission; and then we will figure out how to best broadcast that."

LEVEL 4:

"It's so great you have that relationship to help with that. What did you come up with?"

"Well, we started with my passion for helping women reclaim who they are..."

You can see how the conversation might continue. There might not be a stopping point for a long time. The deeper you go, the more you strengthen your connection. If you commit to the habit of remaining present (it took me lots of counseling to get there) and ask engaging questions that go at least three levels deep, the conversation will be off and running. You can't help but become more connected with your spouse.

B. Counseling

"I love counseling!" said no man, ever.

But counseling can be extremely helpful. I have a business coach; why wouldn't I have a marriage coach? And if you believe that building a connection is the most important habit to conduct in your marriage, what better way to do that than to have a professional moderator for mandatory, scheduled weekly connection sessions?

I promise you, if you do it regularly, it looks nothing like the counseling sessions you see in the movies. More so, it looks like the conversation from the previous section, only with an experienced professional there asking the questions and making sure no one misbehaves during the conversations.

This creates a safe environment in which you and your spouse can share even more true feelings and thoughts. This helps you become even more aligned with the person you have committed to sharing your life with and enables you to build your best life together.

The best part is that often, this financial investment is subsidized by your health insurance plan, and your employer might even allow you to take time off for your counseling sessions. And rightly so, because being proactive about your marriage is one of the best things you can do for all other aspects of your life, including work!

Think about it—who in your organization has gone through a divorce, and how much did that screw up not only their professional lives, but cause stress for all the people around them? It is so much better to be proactive about that relationship and develop great habits. This will give you the capacity to excel in all other areas of your life.

That brings me to my final point: going to counseling doesn't mean something is "wrong." While this is typically the notion others take, I think it is bizarre. When you see a slender or muscular person at the gym, we don't think, "Wow, something must really be wrong with that person that he has stooped so low to go to the gym."

No—instead, we view that person's chiseled physique as the result of spending time in the gym. He is slender or muscular because of lots of work he has put into consistently going to the gym. In the same vein, I think we all can elevate our thinking by being more transparent about our counseling sessions and viewing them as important as spending time working on our physical health.

C. Road Trips

This might seem like an odd subtopic, But I assure you, this is powerful if you bear with me. When is your next road trip? You don't know? OK, go plan one right now. Most of the Perry family's dreams and goals have come from road tripping.

On a road trip, you are trapped within three feet of other people for two, four, eight, or even twenty hours. You are forced to talk to each other. And, if you have done a good job of creating the other habits we've covered, you are all caught up. You know each other. You are connected. There is nothing left to do but dream!

Dream big—talk it out. Pretend this is a strategy session with your executive leadership team at the office. Brainstorm. Say crazy things! This is your life partner. If your kids are old enough, include them, too.

Turn on a podcast or audiobook that aligns with your family's vision. Ask for their thoughts.

Start talking early on the road trip. The conversation will develop and continue through the entire vacation. You will work out problems, create new heights of imagination, and get buy-in from the whole family about your shared purpose.

Then, on the way back, it's time to get tactical. Talk about the whens and the hows, now that you've refreshed your purpose. Put them in your calendar. Send out the emails and texts to the friends, family, and vendors you will need to engage to get rolling. This will ensure that when you arrive back to normal life, the process continues toward your goal.

Tabatha's life-coaching company is the amalgamation of a couple years' worth of road-trip conversations regarding what she wanted to do with her professional life when our kids got older. And here she is now. An entrepreneur. A business owner. A thought leader. A social media influencer. She is on an incredible journey to help successful women reclaim, rediscover, and refine their lives.

So, when is your next family road trip?

2. Parental Habits

Our kids are the next generation. We have been entrusted with shaping the future of our communities and our country. What an awesome responsibility we have!

Many parents feel the stress of parenting on a regular basis. We see this topic filling up our newsfeed on social media, with funny memes in videos that demonstrate passive-aggressive attempts to express our frustrations with our children. Ironically as I'm writing this, I have been interrupted three times in the past two minutes by my children—and admittedly, it is causing me stress.

If we can develop great habits around parenting our children, we can significantly improve our overall capacity and grow our legacy through our kids. There are three strategies I want to share as best practices for developing our habits around our relationships: go on individual "dates" with them, take them on birthday getaways, and express your love for them.

A. Go on Individual "Dates"

What do you think your children want most? The newest toy? The brand-new basketball shoes that their favorite athlete wears? Maybe it's that new car when they turned sixteen?

Sure, all our children want things, but more than all that, they want our time. And more than that, they want our undivided attention with that time.

I have two daughters—Lily, who is six, and Liberty, who is four. They both have significantly different personalities.

Lily is very active and loves playing sports. She loves swimming, running around, ziplining in our backyard, and interacting with her friends. She is meticulously organized. We often find her in a room with a neat arrangement of every toy car and stuffed animal she owns.

Liberty, for lack of a better term, is your typical princess. She loves watching *Frozen* and dressing up as Elsa or Anna. She has an incredible imagination. She is our creative, free-spirited child.

Tabatha and I spend time individually with both girls. I believe the best way to speak to their hearts is through this alone time. This allows us to not only build relationships with our daughters, but also to build credibility with them. We have found that their behavior improves drastically when we have made it a point to spend a lot of time encouraging and interacting with our children individually.

To implement this effectively, it is important to put our individual "dates" on the calendar. Put them in writing. Do *whatever needs to be done* to solidify them and prioritize them. While children are young, they don't need to be elaborate dates. A walk to the park and ten minutes at the playground with Mom or Dad does the trick. Even playing video games with my older daughter, Lily, gives us a special Daddy-daughter bonding time.

The key, though, is that it is planned and executed. If too much time goes by between either of the girls' dates, they start to feel excluded. It's important that the date for each girl takes place on the same day, if possible, or close to it. One of our favorite strategies is for my wife to go on a date with Lily while I go on a date with Liberty.

As far as frequency, I have found that doing this at least monthly—but ideally, weekly—builds momentum in the relationship and truly allows us to bond. I am by no means saying I am executing well on this; in fact, the girls go on a lot more dates with their iPads than they do me. I have a long way to go in this area. The interesting correlation between my parenting and my daughters' behavior is where I experience the most stress in my life.

B. Take Them on Birthday Getaways

Some advice I got recently that I'd like to add is more applicable with older children and I recently implemented it with Lily.

A few months ago, I had the privilege of going to separate dinners with two important people—the CEO of our organization and the COO. Both are incredibly successful fathers who thrive in the bustling New York City lifestyle.

I asked them how they are able to be great fathers to their children amid their demanding schedules. Oddly, they both gave me the same answer: birthday getaways.

Each year on each of their children's birthdays, they take a long weekend and take one child anywhere he or she wants to go—just the two of them.

Wow! What an amazing idea!

This past year, for Lily's fifth birthday, I took the day off work and took her anywhere she wanted to go. We did whatever she wanted to do for the entire day. It was an amazing time. I instantly blocked out all future birthdays from my calendar to make sure that I honor my children on those days. I also implemented this for my wife's birthday and our anniversary.

I cannot wait to have these experiences with my girls over the years. I anticipate they will be some of the most special memories and conversations we ever have!

C. Express Your Love for Them

Finally, I think habits around love are huge capacity builders with our children. Just as with our marriages, when our children feel loved, we build trust with them, and that increases our joint capacity to handle the stress that life throws at us.

How often do you tell your children you love them?

"Well, they know I love them."

Great. So say it! I have never understood the "implied love" model. It's simple to say. So, say it often.

My girls are tired of it. I say it way too much because it's a habit—a habit I believe every parent should adopt.

If you want to open yourself up for feedback, here is a great next-level question to ask your children: "Honey, how do you know that Daddy/Mommy loves you?"

If your child says, "Because you tell me," that's a good thing.

But I challenge you to challenge them to take it to the next level. Follow up with this question: "What does Daddy/Mommy do that lets you know that I love you?"

Whatever their answer is, that's their love language. Do more of that.

The dividends this pays might take decades to realize. But there will be a conversation someday in the future, when you are older, where your children will bring up those moments. They will tell you how much they meant. They will tell you that they shared with their friends growing up how much they knew that their parents loved them.

3. Social Habits

Our last focus is on building capacity by establishing solid habits within our social circles. We all have friends. I have found that these relationships are often based on having a "history" with someone or being in close proximity with one another. I want to challenge you to build habits that create relationships *on purpose*—not just because you've known someone since high school or because someone lives near you or works with you.

Here are three habits you can develop to build the relationships you want: schedule interactions, make intentional choices about who your friends are, and be transparent in all interactions.

A. Schedule Interactions

You probably see a theme—that it's important to schedule habits. If there were a different way that was effective, I would share it. But I know that if I put something in my calendar, there is at least a 70 percent chance that it will happen. If I don't, there is about a 10 percent chance. I like to play the odds.

When it comes to growing your social relationships, plan out and schedule the who, what, where, and when of your interactions.

I encourage you to include your spouse in this habit. Tabatha and I will take inventory of the friends we have and who we want to hang out with, and we put them on a list. Then we will go into our calendars and start shooting off calendar invites and text messages.

This helps us make sure that we don't waste our most precious commodity—time. Specifically, time with one another.

How many hours of the week are you with your spouse? For many people, it's not many. Giving permission for your friends to accompany you during that time should not occur haphazardly but instead be stewarded with the utmost zeal and purpose.

You have my permission and my exhortation to start scheduling interactions and sending out calendar invites to your social events. All of them. And that leads me to the next habit.

B. Make Intentional Choices About Who Your Friends Are

When you make intentional choices about who your friends are, chances are, they will come to love your calendar invites. But they might not love them at first. Talk with them about what is important in a friendship. Also, have that dialogue with your spouse. Here are some questions to discuss:

- Why do we want friends?
- How many friends should we have?
- How many should live within driving distance?
- How many long-distance relationships should we develop?
- Should all our friendships be couples?
- Who do we need to remove from our social list?
- What value can we add to our friends' lives that we're not already?

If you will go through this list of questions with your spouse, you will be well on your way to making intentional choices regarding your social network.

C. Be Transparent in All Relationships

To have deep, meaningful, worth-your-time social relationships, build the habit of making sure all your interactions are transparent.

I think Brené Brown does an amazing job writing and speaking on this topic, and I am a fan of her work. One of her comments that sticks in my mind is that you cannot consider what you are doing as transparent just by saying it is.

We should not have to qualify statements with this "disclaimer." Just jump right into whatever you are going to say.

It certainly takes two to be habitually transparent in a relationship, so it's important to notice whether the other person is reciprocating at a similar level.

When I moved to Texas for a short couple of years, I developed a friendship with a man named Ronnie Cherry. We went to lunch or coffee together maybe eight times during those couple years. But the depth of conversation and the volume of transparency we shared was far beyond most relationships I had previously maintained for decades.

To get there, we shared details about ourselves that went beyond being professional or politically correct. Then the other would reciprocate and go a little further. This process would repeat until we were working through fears, marriage issues, career failures, parenting trials, and other challenges that few others in my life had known about.

The key is to be the one who instigates transparency, early and often. And then take stock of how the other reciprocates. If you find that you can alternate drilling deeper, the relationship is a keeper! With this habit built inside your relationships like this, you can be sure to call on that person when you start to feel stressed and enter the breakdown cycle

If you have explored these cycles with them before, this relationship just may be the one you need to encourage you to push toward breakthrough in your capacity, and on your way to building your best life!

Chapter 10: "Doing" Habits

The final set of habits that will increase your capacity to handle stress is the "doing" habits. They are action-oriented and probably absorb most of your time. Winning in these categories can have a significant impact on building your capacity ceiling.

The most important doing habits we will focus on are your vocational habits, avocational habits, and financial habits.

1. Vocational Habits

Your *vocation* refers to what you do for a living. How do you provide an income for your household? We have all heard the phrase, "If you love what you do, you will never work a day in your life." This may be true, but there are things that you still must do to build capacity around your vocation.

The steps in this process are to define and live according to your purpose, do calendaring consistently.

A. Define and Live According to Your Purpose—Your "Why"

Your *purpose* is your "why." Simon Sinek's book *Start with Why* was a transformational book in my life. After I read this book, our organization went on a three-month journey identifying a common "why" that we could unite around. Doing this will give you an incredible amount of energy if you align with that purpose and live according to it once you've identified it.

The energy will fuel your ability to build habits around other key tactical aspects of your vocation.

To identify our organization's "why," we met as a leadership team. Even if you do not lead an organization, this can be a powerful exercise to do on your own. When you fully articulate your purpose, it creates a framework for decision making that allows you additional capacity in building your (or your organization's) best life!

Our leadership team discussed the reason why identifying our purpose was important. I read to everyone an outline of Sinek's book so we could start off on the same page. We decided that to find our "why," we needed to state our collective mission, vision, values, and beliefs.

I could write an entire book on the meaning and importance of each of these, but I won't go into that much detail here. I specifically want to address the crafting of a mission.

i. We wrote, shared, and refined drafts. To start, each individual member of our senior leadership team created their own version of what we thought the mission should be for our organization.

Then we shared and defended our thoughts with the whole team. From these, we identified keywords that appeared in most of the phrases we had all identified, and we made a list. From that list, we all individually went back to the drawing board to craft a second draft with a common set of phrases.

Once we had all completed our second drafts, we read them aloud and recorded them together. After parting company, I, as the leader, took all the phrases and wordsmithed them into a single statement. Doing this alone allowed the rest of the group to ruminate on the conversation and personally clarify what was most meaningful to them, without the natural drift of "groupthink." We reunited and then tore that apart until we had something we all agreed on as our mission.

ii. We took our draft mission statement to key stakeholders. I conducted nearly a dozen one-on-one sessions with some of the leading members of our organization who are not on the management team and asked for their feedback. I shared with them what we had come up with. I asked what they liked, what they would change, and what they would add. This gave us much more food for thought.

iii. Third, we invited everyone else in our organization to weigh in. We held a large focus group in which we revealed our newly tweaked mission and then provided some of the additional feedback we had been given. We recorded the feedback in the cases where people had differing views, specifically identifying new verbiage they liked. We also noted the unanimous consensus on certain components.

Next, I took all these notes, reconstructed the final draft to include all the components that were heavily weighted, and took it to our leadership team for final approval.

Here is the mission statement for our organization that emerged from that process:

"We live to lead others into building their best life!"

This was a powerful summation that most people felt very strongly about.

That was the easy part.

iv. We ingrained the statement into our daily lives. This was the most difficult task. We have taken several steps to do this as an organization. I want to share a couple that I highly recommend you do with your mission.

One habit we have is at the beginning of each group session, we put our mission up on the board. We ask four people to share a story about where and how they have witnessed this concept being lived out over the previous several days. This, by far, has been the most powerful ingraining tool for our culture.

As an individual, you could begin each day by reading your life's mission and then journaling one way that you observed it or experienced it lived out in the past twenty-four hours.

Next, we plastered our mission statement everywhere. We displayed it in all our slide shows, on computer desktops, in posters on walls, in slides on digital signage, in recruiting videos—you name it, it's everywhere. We often read it out loud. This gives it power and purpose. It creates permanency and legitimacy.

And then we were purposeful about building professional relationships only with people whose "why" aligned with ours. What more powerful way to instill something into yourself and your culture than to create new relationships only with people whose "why" aligns with yours! This creates a commanding flywheel effect.

We use our mission statement to govern. Whenever there is conflict, we refer to our mission and align our actions with the greater "why". If we deviate from this, we course-correct and realign.

All these habits in identifying and calling our purpose, when done right, give us the energy we need to execute on the following other important habits.

B. Do Calendaring Consistently

You are probably wondering why it took me so long to get to a full section titled "Calendaring." It has been heavily seasoned throughout the book already. The most important place that calendaring shows up though, is in your vocational habits. I want to give you a quick rundown on how to build amazing habits around creating significant capacity in your work life with your calendar.

The first thing I do is create an *ideal* schedule. Ideal being the key term. This means if everything went perfectly, this is how your week would go. You must understand this will never happen, so don't feel like you fail when you don't accomplish it. The goal is to get 70-80% of it done, which means you will be three to five times more effective than someone without this calendar.

I like to use an excel spreadsheet to build this out first before going into my Outlook calendar. I create thirty minutes time increments down the left side of the page and daily headers along the top. I then create boxes of time of all the things I need to get done, understanding that each cell represents thirty minutes.

I then start with the most important components, the nonnegotiables. Things like exercise, eating, when I wake up, and my revenue-generating activities. I start the game of Tetris as I place blocks in throughout my day. I try to never schedule more than two hours' worth of continuous activity without allowing for a break. These breaks are key to maintaining high levels of productivity.

The next step is to then take this ideal schedule in excel, after it has all been fit together, and put it into my calendaring system. I use Outlook personally, but you can use whatever you like. I put all the items in there just as they are listed in the spreadsheet, with names, addresses, and subject matter. This allows for maximum organization and preparedness so that when the day hits, all I must do is execute.

Typically, on Sunday night, I will go in and preview my upcoming week. I will reconcile any double bookings, which are typically calendar invites I have received from others, and note any breaks or gaps in my calendar that have developed.

I also like to color-code my calendar. So, each type of activity gets a color-code. Be creative! Come up with your own categories and colors. A final habit I associate with this is that each time something doesn't happen in my calendar, I color code it a bright red. This way, I can reconcile my percentage of completion toward my ideal schedule. This allows me to be more precise next quarter when I remodel my ideal schedule.

C. Master Your Vocation

It is also extremely important to build mastery around your vocation. Just like "leaders are readers" because they are constantly trying to elevate their ability to effectively lead, you must continue to perfect your craft.

I am reminded of a time I watched another business leader post a Facebook live video where he was training his receptionist on how to answer the phone.

For fifteen minutes, they practiced that ever typical, "Thank you for calling ACME Corporation, how may I direct your call?"

Over and over, they drilled this so that the pitch of every syllable matched the culture that they wanted to portray to all the people they encountered in their business.

This level of meticulous mastery struck a nerve in my brain. How could I continue to sharpen the saw and build muscle memory around the most important components of my job?

I go back to the ideal schedule and ask you, is there time in there for *getting better* at what you do? If there isn't, there should be. Thirty minutes a day or a couple hour blocks a week. Put that time in there. Then decide what you can work on perfecting in that time that will have the biggest impact on you living out your mission.

For me, I have found this is typically language. What we say when we interact with prospects, talent, or coaching our internal people. We can always be improving and elevating this experience for the end-user. Drilling this on a regular basis allows us to maximize every interaction that we have.

2. Avocational Habits

An *avocation* is an activity we spend on that is unrelated to what we do for a living. Building solid habits around an avocation helps us thrive in our vocations. These habits are to unplug, make time for recreation, and find opportunities to serve others. Building these habits creates significant capacity in our lives.

A. Unplug

The analogy is so simple. What happens to your phone if you don't plug it in and charge it? It dies—it literally turns off. And what does your phone contain? If you're like me, it contains almost all the information I need to grow my business. If I had to, I could operate most of a multimillion-dollar organization from this little block.

We are exactly the opposite of our phones. If we don't unplug, we can't recharge. We run out of power to operate. We can become so stressed that we can no longer run in an effective capacity. Our brain, just a little blob in our head, is what makes us capable of operating our entire life. Without unplugging, it is in danger of turning off.

One of the most important habits I use to "unplug" relates to my phone. When I get home from work, I take my phone into my room and put it on the charger, and then I head back downstairs. That way, I cannot be tempted by all the "important" things that are going to surface that can certainly wait until the morning. This one habit significantly enhances my ability to be present with my family and to recharge from a day that I accomplished at a pace of a million miles an hour.

This nightly unplugging is a mini-vacation that helps me build my ability to operate at a high level the next day. An additional relationship-based capacity-building by-product is that it also allows me to be completely present with my wife and children.

I also believe we should take this concept to the next level a couple of times a year. Take a long weekend trip with your spouse or by yourself. Go somewhere that has no cell-phone reception. Watch a movie, take lots of walks, and journal on paper or on a laptop, if necessary. The rule is no internet or cell phone for the bulk of the day, for at least three days.

B. Make Time for Recreation

"What do you do for fun?"

For years, when people would ask me this question, I would answer, "Business." And while it was the truth, it wasn't healthy. There are seasons for more work and less play, but the word "season" implies there is a beginning and an end. Identify the *season* if you are calling it one.

Our family recently moved to Minnesota, and this provided a natural new season in my life. I decided I wanted to build time into my schedule for recreation—specifically, I wanted to get back into basketball.

So I signed up for a membership at a gym that has basketball courts and then asked about open gyms. I started attending them. It was embarrassing at first because I was temporarily living in an area of town wrought with talented basketball players, and I was just trying to get back in shape. But slowly, over time, I built up the stamina to get up and down the court so I could then focus on reestablishing my skills.

I also kept telling people that I played basketball. This allowed me to have more dimensions to my conversations than kids and work, and it gave other people an opportunity to invite me to play in their groups. This was fun because it created new relationships. Ultimately, I found the group that I play with three times a week now.

I can't tell you how much capacity this has built into my life. It provided content for this book, gave me analogies for my organization, gave me the ability to run up and down a court for two hours straight without stopping, brought me referral partners, helped me acquire talent, gave me competitive release, led to weight loss, lowered my blood pressure—the list goes on.

For many years in the name of "building a business," I missed out on this amazing component of my life. As you build your capacity, you will discover that your time will open for these activities you have always "wished" you could incorporate into your schedule.

C. Find Opportunities to Serve Others

Just like sending out encouraging messages to people is a great way to turn around a bad day, the habit of serving on a regular basis creates much capacity to handle crappy things that happen in your life. When you are put in a position to help people or organizations that need service, it forces you to reconcile how blessed you truly are. This reflection typically produces thankfulness, which, in turn, allows you to significantly reduce, if not eliminate, stress that stems from what you feel like you don't have.

Being actively involved in our church provides ample opportunity for me to serve. My wife and I serve on the security team and prayer team. We also lead small-group studies and provide a forum and encouragement for others to build their best lives.

Our church has a local and global heart for serving, so several times a year, we organize events. For example, for several hours on a Saturday, we all join to accomplish a task that benefits our community. We have found these to be fun yet impactful events to be involved in, and we try to select events that our young children can be involved in so they develop a heart for serving.

I have heard many people voice that they "don't know where to serve."

This is a poor excuse. If you are not involved in some type of church, and your workplace doesn't regularly serve its community, I suggest writing down three things you enjoy doing. Then do a Google search for that word and add "volunteer." I know you will find areas to serve immediately. And I promise you that the capacity you personally build from this habit will be as valuable to you as it will be to the people who are impacted by your service.

When you serve individuals and organizations that are less fortunate than you are, it gives you a fresh perspective on your life that increases your capacity. You realize how blessed you are, and that can eradicate stress caused by comparatively trivial concerns.

3. Financial Habits

Finances drive so many other components of our lives. Our habits in this area determine our capacity to operate well within other areas. If you had a sky-high capacity level, financially speaking, how well would you be crushing it? What do you need to do differently?

Four important habits to adopt so you can start with winning financially are to define your vision, develop and follow a budget, build a contentment circle, and give to others.

A. Define Your Vision

Just like we need to create a mission and then habits around incorporating our mission into our vocations, it is important that we have a financial vision for our lives as well. Lots of people think vision is a destination you can arrive at, but this is a mistake. It's a journey.

My favorite definition for *vision* is "what life looks like on the journey to our mission."

My mission in life is to be a devoted financial steward, helping grow the Kingdom of God through missions and evangelism work. Being a financial steward means I must pay special attention to how I handle my finances. My vision is to be able to give $100 million per year to this cause someday.

All these are just milestones toward achieving the greater vision. After we determine our financial priorities, then we need to determine how much we need, build a plan for making that amount, and then figuring out how much it is appropriate to want (see the upcoming discussion about contentment circles). This strategy provides the framework for creating a budget to live by.

B. Develop and Follow a Budget

Ahhhh, everyone's favorite topic—budgets! I have had a love/hate relationship with budgets, but ultimately, I realize they provide freedom.

Having a budget makes the decision for me as to whether I can or can't do something. It means I don't have to have an in-depth philosophical discussion with myself (or my wife) each time I want to deploy capital.

Tabatha and I found that while we were still in debt, a budget was significantly more crucial than when we had eliminated our debt. After we eliminated that debt, we then had more freedom to spend money where needed. We established automatic savings and investment strategies.

At the height of our debt-eradication season, we would review our weekly spending and the corresponding budgeted allowance for each category on Sunday evenings. We would then plan out our spending for the next week and shuffle allowances around to ensure we did not exceed the total expense allotment for the month. Then, at the beginning of each new month, we would create a plan for our upcoming expenses.

Building this habit gave us an easy-to-follow framework for building capacity in our financial lives.

BONUS: AN AMAZON SPENDING HACK

Tabatha and I found that our Amazon purchases were some of the most challenging to rein in. Not only was it difficult to delineate the categories for them; it was so easy to purchase *needed* items all the time.

You have probably noticed this if your front porch is littered with Amazon boxes *every single day*. To help limit this, we have incorporated a new rule that we both enjoy playing by: we load up the Amazon cart all week long with whatever we feel like we want, whenever we want it. Then on Sunday, we review all those items together, eliminate items we changed our mind about, and order the rest.

Rarely did one spouse have to talk to the other out of purchasing something unnecessary. We usually came to that conclusion on our own. This resulted in a roughly 70 percent reduction in our monthly Amazon spending.

Try it! Then you might have enough money to buy one of your friends a copy of this book! (Just make sure you keep it in your shopping cart until Sunday).

C. Create a Contentment Circle

I first heard about this concept in a book whose title I do not recall. This lack of reconcilable detail is an admitted downside of listening to Audible.com books on two times the normal speed. The good part is, I made up my own concept of a contentment circle. Here it is.

Because you have purchased this book and are going to now grow your capacity exponentially, I know you will move further down the road towards living your best life! This increased success can lead to more financial inflow into your life. It is important to avoid the 'lifestyle creep" that so quickly follows this increase in inflow.

Lifestyle creep refers to the incremental luxuries you continuously introduce to your life as you make more money. Examples include ordering drinks with dinner; ordering appetizers with your drinks; and going to one restaurant for drinks, another for appetizers and drinks, another for drinks and dinner, and another for dessert. These are not bad things, necessarily, but they add up.

This seemingly innocuous example of lifestyle creep gets even more pronounced when you start incorporating housing, big toys, vehicles, and other indulgences. The problem is that your marginal utility, or the "extra happiness" you get from these expenses, pales in comparison to the percentage increase in monetary spending. My solution is the *contentment circle*.

To create your contentment circle, take a notepad and write out all the things you want in your best life. Jot down everything—the toys, the house, the cars, the jewelry, the services, the schooling. Write down everything that costs money in your dream life. Then have your spouse do the same. Next, combine the lists. Draw a circle around it.

Finally, make a covenant with yourself and your spouse that *this is it!* Nothing more can creep into the list. You just described the maximum lifestyle you will allow yourself to create. Right now, it seems luxurious and opulent. I can promise you, someday when you get there, it will seem rather ordinary. Stick to the contentment circle, and you will increase your capacity.

D. Give to Others

Once you have achieved obtaining all of the items in your contentment circle, and it will happen sooner than you think, you are faced with a decision on what to do with all of the extra. Give it away. Give away the excess capital that you normally would have spent on lifestyle creep. Nothing has a higher return on investment than generosity. Biblically, Christians are called to give a tithe (10 percent) of their income back to God. There is so much wisdom to be gained from first giving to others before consuming for yourself.

Create this habit now, and you will spend the rest of your life in financial bliss. Your capacity is so large, and you will have so much margin, that you can't help but be filled with joy!

Part 4: Relationships

The final area that you need to grow to increase your capacity is your relationships. We will discuss many different types of relationships in the following pages. I want you to think about all of them like this: there is someone, somewhere, at some point in time, who can help you out of any situation you find yourself in.

Please think about that for a minute.

When was the last time you felt stressed? For me, it was this morning. Yes, the guy writing the book on handling stress well feels stress, too. I was feeling stressed because I looked at my calendar and saw that I had sixteen meetings scheduled for the day. It was a busy day, for sure. Back-to-back thirty-minute meetings all day long! (This book author doesn't always follow his own advice of scheduling regular breaks into his calendar.)

How could a relationship help me with this? Well, let's look at the different components of my sixteen meetings. How many did I *have* to conduct in an ideal world?

Six of those meetings were coaching sessions for members of our leadership team and new agents we had hired. If I had hired a strong sales or leadership coach on retainer, they could have executed these sessions much more effectively than me.

Two of those meetings were group training sessions for my advisors. I could have easily delegated this responsibility to a strong, charismatic leader inside our organization.

One meeting was a group presentation that a strong recruiter in our office could have handled.

Look at that—I could have removed more than half the meetings from my plate by delegating them if I had taken the time to develop the proper relationships prior to this morning.

Relationships are key to increasing our capacity to handle all that happens in life.

In the following chapters, I explore the two main types of relationships we develop: professional and personal.

Chapter 11: Professional Relationships

There are several types of professional relationships. I want you to think about them as any relationship that could help you advance in your vocation—what you do to make money in this world.

You might have already identified some of these relationships. But you may have holes in this list. After reviewing it, you might realize that you want to replace some of the people and choose others who can better satisfy this relationship.

Be intentional in each of these areas. When you say "Yes" to someone, that means you are saying "No" to someone else. You can't be all things to everyone. Let's dive in.

1. Coaches, Managers, and Mentors

One important type of relationship is the one you have with your life or career coach or manager. The relationships you will have with different coaches and managers can look a lot alike. These people should hold a high place of authority and respect in your life. If they do, you will want to spend as much time with them as you can.

A coach is typically someone you or your company hires, so you have no reporting relationship with him or her, vocationally. A coach should be solely focused on what you want to accomplish, what your vision is for the future, and helping you get there. He or she should ask lots of questions but not always provide the answers for you.

A manager is someone you might say you "work for." This is someone you might not necessarily get to pick, but when you have a good one, you do everything you can to remain on his or her team. Good managers will do everything they can to get you promoted. If given the choice between working for a good manager for less pay and working for a poor manager for more pay, I believe the best choice is to choose the good manager. This person will help build your best life, not just make sure you get paid a little more in the short term.

Great professional mentors do not come around often. These are people who have successfully been there, done that, and are now focused on significance. They want to help you get to where they have been, only faster and with less painful mistakes. You might engage formally and meet on a regular basis, or you can keep it casual and just participate in ad hoc (specific) conversations.

Look for a coach or mentor with gray hair. As people get closer to the end of their for-profit careers, they strive to have an impact on what and whom they leave behind. Treat this relationship like gold.

2. An Accountability Partner

It is not possible for us to hold ourselves fully accountable. But we must *be* accountable. This means we must establish relationships with people we can be accountable to—account-ability partners.

This can be more difficult than it sounds. If the person you are accountable to takes his or her criticism over the top, you might lose respect for that person or feel discouraged when you fail and, as a result, limit your engagement. If the person is too casual with you, then it will be difficult to attain an optimal result, and you might lose steam.

You will probably develop different accountability relationships in your life for different goals. I reached a point where I hadn't written more content for this book in more than a month. I was headed on a family vacation for a week, and on the drive out, I asked my wife to ask me each day how my writing was going. I set a goal of writing 1,500 words per day on that trip for seven days.

She, of course, agreed, but she had to ask me only once. This is what *being accountable* looks like. Pick the right person with the right plan, get his or her buy-in, and you will accomplish your goal.

3. Your Peers

Peers are our counterparts throughout whatever community we identify. Some people might consider them our *equals*, but I don't like to use that label. To be someone's *equal* means you must compare yourself with others. I believe comparison robs your joy. Comparing, while often well-intentioned, ultimately means one person gets torn down for the benefit of lifting another up.

Instead, I think we should look at peers as the people who have the same titles as us, are in close proximity to us, or are in the same stage of life. I encourage you to seek out peers who have components in their lives that you can, and want to, emulate. Notice, I didn't say that their lives are "enviable."

Everyone is good at something. Pick a character trait of someone around you that you would like to improve in your life—and then start to spend time with them.

One of my peers, also named Steve, is one of the most positive, encouraging people I know. We have similar titles and work experience, and we are both fathers of two young children. I talk to Steve several times a week, even though he lives one thousand miles away. I always leave our conversations refreshed and encouraged.

This enhancement to my mindset allows me to pass on the infectious trait known as *optimism* to the people I will meet later that day. When I am able to pass this encouragement on to others, it adds a layer to my capacity pillar. By focusing on others, I build relational capital that I can call on later, when I need encour-agement.

When we select growth-minded peers to relate to and interact with regularly, we can't help but grow our capacity ceiling.

4. Your Advocates

Everyone needs an advocate. You have only twenty-four hours in a day, and you can be in only one place at a time. The world is full of people whom, at any given time, you are not influencing. We grow our impact exponentially and fulfill significance by having advocates out there on our behalf.

In my professional life, we call these important people "centers of influence." They are people who want to see you be successful, and typically, they have some type of a vested interest in your success. Your being *successful* means that they are being *significant*. This results when you work toward aligning your vocational habits with your core purpose.

Seek out people who meet others you can help on a regular basis. Who or what does your business help accomplish? What problems does it solve? Who meets those people on a regular basis, outside your work?

Find those people, and develop relationships with them. They will consistently connect you with people you can help. As a result, you will increase your ability to handle stress because you will have more new, profitable connections than you know what to do with. These people will become your network—people you helped, people who have helped you, and the connectors in the middle.

Bill Cates talks about this in his book *Radical Relevance*. In his work, he does an incredible job of encouraging us to connect with other people. He explains how when you give, you get. Those connections will return the favor by connecting you with countless introductions.

It all starts with being valuable in other's lives first. Build your best life by helping others build theirs.

5. Business/Industry Leaders

I have always prided myself on not being afraid to talk to or reach out to anyone.

As you are growing in your industry, you will start to recognize leaders whom you are attracted to. My advice is to reach out to them.

Today, this is easier than it has ever been. Typically, the higher people rise in their careers, the easier it is to find their contact information online. Search for them on their company websites or on their personal websites. You could also find them on social media and identify mutual contacts, or just reach out to them directly.

In your message to them, it is important to be clear about why you are reaching out. Here are a couple pointers for crafting the perfect message:

1. Be respectful in your message.

2. Reference a common connection—a person, a company, a location, or an alumni status.

3. Tell them something specific you admire about their leadership style or accomplishments.

4. Relate that back to how you want to grow yourself.

5. Don't make them ask what you hope to accomplish. Tell them exactly what you would like to talk about and how long you would like to talk about it.

You might have to reach out more than once. It is important to be persistent—but be professional in your persistence.

Once they have agreed to a meeting, I always prepare an agenda for the meeting. I list all the questions and topics I would like to discuss and then distill it down to the most important ones. I then send an email a few days before our meeting to outline the items I would like to discuss in more detail so they can prepare.

Using this method, I have been able to visit with seven- and eight-figure business leaders, executives with Fortune 100 companies, professional athletes, and more.

I have rarely called on these relationships for a specific need. I think the biggest benefit is the confidence that I could connect with them—and the benefits that come from being confident.

Always value the advice you are given in those sessions. Much like mentors, these professionals have been where you want to go. If you can learn from other people's mistakes, you can limit or avoid them and arrive at your future vision faster. This, in turn, gives you the opportunity to continue to develop an even larger vision—and more capacity.

Go ahead, dream big!

Chapter 12: Personal Relationships

Personal relationships are those you have with all the people who are outside your vocation. We get to choose some of them, while others are chosen for us. Intentionality is extremely important in developing these relationships.

You will find that these will probably be the most dynamic relationships in your life. You will go through seasons when you will invest in one type of personal relationships more than others.

For example, when my second daughter, Liberty, was born, we had recently moved three thousand miles from our home. We were far away from family and had limited relationships in our new community. During this season, it was particularly important that I focus on my relationships with Tabatha and our kids. I had to intentionally put on hold developing new social relationships. Also, I wasn't mentoring anyone at the time, nor did I have the capacity to.

To some, this might seem to come naturally. However, I assure you, it is essential to do it on purpose. If I had neglected developing my relationship with Tabatha, she would have felt even more isolated than a new mother normally does. These situations can be dangerous for people. Sleep deprivation can turn into depression, which, in turn, can lead to prescription drug dependence and result in addiction, divorce—or even worse.

Besides loving my wife and children and wanting to spend the time with them, this intentional focus on relationship building with them helped me avoid potential severe, long-term consequences that didn't align with my ideal envisioned future.

My previous hyperbole went from mundane to extreme quickly. However, I imagine you know someone who has chemical dependence or has been divorced. What was the catalyst? Could a well-developed, intentional, personal relationship have prevented that? Building our capacity is not just a nicety; the breakdown cycle is real. You have two choices: breakdown or breakthrough.

In the following pages, I share examples of how developing relationships with others in your personal life can help you significantly increase your capacity.

1. Your Spouse

My personal opinion is that, other than your relationship with God, your relationship with your spouse is the most important in your life. This is the person whom you made a covenant with and commit to spending the rest of your life with.

So many people in society view marriage as an "us vs. them" relationship—wrought with conflict and strife. The irony is thick, considering you probably spent months or years trying to woo this person, culminating in spending the equivalent to a down payment on your first house (or maybe your actual down payment) on a ring. Did you celebrate your union with that person with a five-figure-price-tag party? Did you do all that only to begin to describe them immediately as "the ol' ball and chain"?

No, I refuse to let this happen. Our household doesn't allow us to say "divorce." Not even in jest has that word ever come out of Tabatha's mouth or mine. We constantly remind each other that we are "on the same team."

Recently, I received a call from a critical member of our team. This person was the entry point for sourcing, recruiting, and onboarding every new person into our organization—truly the linchpin. It was one of those calls that is short. It started like this:

"I need to talk to you."

I have gotten those calls before, and I wish my mind didn't go where it does, but instantly I knew. I knew she had gotten another job offer and was considering quitting.

Where did I turn first? It wasn't to another coworker. It was my wife, my partner in life. She had already been through this with me before, and we made it through just fine, but she didn't say that. What she said was this:

"I will do whatever you need me to do to help. If I must come in and start recruiting and work for you, I will. Whatever you need!"

This was coming from a woman who had weeks prior finally realized a dream of starting her own business, emerging from SAHM (stay-at-home momhood), and was eagerly anticipating the excitement ahead of her. Coming to work for me was the last thing she wanted to do.

Her willingness to self-sacrifice to help me and the relationship we had built took all the anxiety away as I entered that meeting with one of my most important team members.

It gave me the confidence to know that, regardless of the result, we were going to succeed through it. My relationship-based capacity ceiling exceeded the stress level that this situation rose to, and I was able to handle it well.

Thank you, Tabatha!

2. Your Kids

Your kids are your legacy. You are blessed to have them. I am so thankful that my wife and I did not have any challenges getting pregnant. I view my kids as an opportunity to make my impact on the world in a great way!

However, they are tough! Children can bring the best and worst out of you. They certainly can do that to me. I think it is important to repeat something I said at the beginning of this book: to move toward "breakthrough" and increase your capacity ceiling, you need to improve your education, habits, and relationships.

You need to improve your relationships. So, while we certainly can develop new ones, improving the ones we have, has a huge effect on our ability to handle stress.

How do we improve our relationships with our kids? Well, I discussed a few habits earlier in the book that you can adopt. But I really think it comes down to our mindset. Sometimes I feel like parents forget we are responsible for our children's development. We can never let that happen.

A few minutes ago, I went in to use the restroom. Currently working from home, I have adopted the use of my daughters' restroom because it is closest to my makeshift office.

As I entered, I thought, *"What a mess! Why don't they clean this up?"*

Now, the good parents out there are laughing at that, but— being slow at times—I had that thought. Fortunately, I was able to realize that this was my fault. I had allowed the kids to leave the bathrooms a mess. I had not shown them what my expectations were regarding the cleanliness of their bathroom.

The stress I was starting to feel because of the disorderly bathroom was quickly diminished because of my next thought, which was empowering "I have influence over this relationship. I can help develop and mold my girls into clean human beings. And I get to do that in a loving way."

The empowerment that comes from being in relationship with and close proximity to your children naturally creates margin between your capacity and where you are now. Grow these relationships, and it will significantly impact your legacy.

3. Your Extended Family

Your extended family is potentially a very influential component of your relationships, or not. I think this is really the first area where you have decisions to make. These aren't your spouse and your kids, to whom you have a responsibility to develop and increase your relationship, no matter what. Instead, you have the option.

If you are an adult, this also applies to your parents and siblings.

So, what is the framework to look at when choosing to develop and increase your relationships with the rest of your (and your spouse's) family?

First, remember that you have only twenty-four hours in a day and 365 days in a year. You have probably already passively or actively delegated that time to be spent on something. Thus, if you choose to add something else, like spending time with your wife's third cousin, Bubba, drinking beer, you are saying "No" to something else in your life.

If you are serious about intentionality and growing your capacity, which I know you are because you are reading this book, then you need to take stock of your extended family, just like you would with your social relationships. You *do* have a choice. You have no obligation to spend time with them just because a few generations ago, you had the same last name.

Notice, I said "spend time." This goes along with the point I made earlier: you can invest time, and you can spend it. When you *invest* time, you hope to gain a return that is more than what you put into it. Think of a win–win proposition. But when you *spend* time, it's like spending money—you obtain something that, in the moment, was worth what it took you to obtain that money.

Make sure that when you are choosing which members of your family to build relationships with, it is an investment—not an expense.

That brings me to my final point. I am not asking you to put up all the pictures of your extended family on a wall like an *America's Most Wanted* display, and then circle the ones you feel can bring the most value to you and strategically help you get something you want—although that could be a by-product of your relationship with some of them.

Instead, I am saying that you will want those people to reciprocate your investment in the relationship. The sum of your investment of time together should equal two times or more. If there is a deficiency in reciprocity in the relationship, then consider whether you want to continue.

This can be tricky, but it you navigate it successfully, you can avoid a lot of stress and pain. When you take a strategic approach to growing your relationship with your family, you can create huge capacity.

4. Your Social Circle

Social relationships are likely where you spend most of your time working on developing relationships. We have so many options on where to identify and grow these relationships. It could be co-workers that become out of work friends, fellow churchgoers, neighbors, our kids' friends' parents. This list goes on and on.

So how do we choose? What portion of our *relationship-building hours* should we allocate toward this? How do we know when to end a relationship?

I like to think about this a lot like dating. Most of us have had good experiences and bad experiences with dating. We have all had experiences. I want to share a story about some coaching I gave a colleague of mine at one point.

"Joe" had kept going on dates with people and was disappointed with the caliber of individuals he found on the other end of the relationship. They were never serious about their careers. They didn't know what their goals were in life. They lived for the weekend, surrounding themselves with people who talked about fashion, sports, and the news. At the end of each date, they typically had "one too many drinks."

Joe was frustrated because he wanted to find someone he could build his best life with. He sought a true partner who was going to encourage him in the tough times, challenge him to grow, and live a full and significant life with him. Why couldn't he find someone like this to date?

My first and last question to him was, "Where are you looking for this person?"

Have you ever heard the phrase "Consider the source"? What do you think Joe's answer to me was?

"Tinder, the bar, Snapchat," and some other hookup apps disguised as dating apps. Those sources were marketed as giving the results he was achieving. Unsurprisingly, he was met with shallow, insignificant, and imminently doomed relationships.

So my advice was, "Let's start with the source. Where does the type of person you want to spend time with invest her time?"

"The gym."

"Great. What time do they get to the gym?"

"Early."

"Right. Where else do these women congregate?"

"Work."

"Agreed. They are probably pretty motivated to advance in their careers. But you can't just start waltzing into various places of business and ask to be introduced to the most motivated females in there, can you?"

"That would be tough," Joe said.

"So, where or what else does this ideal person invest her time?"

"Church, other volunteer organizations, professional networking groups?"

"Is that a question?"

"No, sorry. That is definitely where they spend time."

"So should you. Tell me your plan."

I tell this story because it is the same approach we should establish when looking to grow our social relationships. Like Joe and his dating, we should be intentional in where we and with whom we spend our time.

Be intentional, deliberate, calculated, and goal-oriented. Find the places where the people you want to surround yourself with congregate, and then implant yourself there. Then all you have to do is connect.

5. Your Mentee

A lot of my relationship-building advice up to this point has been about how you can grow *your* capacity, for *yourself.* I want to stress that, even when you identify connections that are influential in helping build yourself properly, all your relationships will be building capacity for both you and them. If you are not giving and putting in just as much or more into these relationships, the other people will eventually decide it is not a great investment of their time to continue to spend time with you.

So I suggest that most of your relationships involve both parties pouring into it. You should also have a few relationships whose entire goal is for you to mentor or pour into the other person, to help them realize their potential. The key here is *potential.* They may not be able to reciprocate the value you bring to the relationship immediately, but they should have the *potential* to do so. They should be growth-minded and on a journey of building their best life. Through your mentorship, you will see them start to build capacity that will someday blossom into them leading others into building their best lives.

Then you will, either directly or indirectly, realize the return on the investment of your time in mentoring them. You will have the satisfaction of knowing that you have been significant in their lives and in the lives of the people that they touch.

Now, think of three people in your life:

1. Someone who had a big impact on your life more than ten years ago

2. Someone you know who is having a tough time in life right now

3. Someone you are proud of.

Now, I want you to send each of them an encouraging text message. It should be specific, and it should be at least five lines long.

OK, do it.

Do it now.

How do you feel? Encouraged? Uplifted?

Whenever I do that, I feel like Mother Theresa, as if I had just spent my entire life sacrificing for the betterment of society. I'm slightly exaggerating, but honestly, you can't help but leave that exercise encouraged and motivated to continue growing yourself into the best version you can be.

That is capacity building. That is what happens when you establish a regular mentoring role with someone else.

So where do you find someone to mentor? It would be a little awkward to walk up to someone who looks like he or she needs a mentor, whatever that looks like, and say, "I want to mentor you."

How do you do it properly?

You need to be in proximity with people who are in an earlier season of their life than you. Earlier I talked about developing a habit of serving on a regular basis. My experience is that these mentoring relationships often develop from when you are serving. The great part about serving is that it is a social and status equalizer. College students pack meal kits next to CEO's, elected officials sweep trash next to construction laborers.

I have a few examples of where some of my mentoring relationships have developed from. First, I spent several years coaching youth basketball teams. Next, I volunteered to be a chaperone for a high school short term missions team. Finally, I regularly volunteer to pray with people after church.

Each of these has produced relationships with others who I am able to encourage, coach, listen to, and build relationships with people who are in earlier seasons in their life and are looking for someone to mentor them.

6. Take Your Shot!

What does that mean? This is the fun part. Today's digital world provides more access than ever to go straight to people at the top of their game.

Think of a list of the top ten people you would love to connect with and build a relationship with. If you were to develop a relationship with any one person on this list, it would catapult your growth.

So, what are you waiting for? Do it. Build the list. Then come up with a strategy to try and connect. I can promise you it isn't going to happen by accident. They aren't going to look for you and try and connect with you. So, this is in your control.

Let me give you a couple examples.

A few years ago, I was in a local leadership cohort sponsored by my city's chamber of commerce. There was an intensive application process, and a committee of previous members selected the participants. I had just moved to town, so I certainly had no connections. I knew it would be a great place to develop relationships, so I applied.

I was initially denied. Talk about an ego buster! But I received a last-minute phone call before the program began. One of the committee members told me I had been an alternate, and a position opened up. I had to humble myself and accept my *last-place* entry into the group.

I am so glad I did. I developed amazing new connections and learned much about the community I was new to.

Once a month, we would gather and spend an entire day together being bussed around town, learning about different areas of the community—government, sports, agriculture, manufacturing. It was an experience like no other, and I am very thankful for it.

On one of these days, we had the privilege of having one of the most famous professional basketball players from the '90s come speak to our group. She had grown up in the area and agreed to share some insights and stories with us. I had grown up admiring this person—particularly the basketball shoes she had produced with a top shoe manufacturer.

At the end of the sports icon's presentation, she asked the audience if we had questions. I knew what I wanted to say, but an intense fear of rejection welled up inside me. I didn't want to be inappropriate or unprofessional. But I knew this was a chance to take a shot. I felt the fear and did it anyway.

I raised my hand.

"Yes?"

"Hi, my name is Steven Perry. I grew up playing basketball and love your shoe designs! I always wanted a pair but was never able to get them. Any chance they will ever be released again?"

"Well, thank you so much," the basketball legend said. Those were my pride and joy. It was so much fun being able to help design and develop those. It's funny you ask; we are working on releasing them again. What size do you wear?"

"Nine and a half."

"Well, then, I will personally get you a pair when they come back out this summer."

I had taken my shot. The ball was headed toward the hoop but hadn't arrived yet. That was just the first step. I made a connection, differentiated myself, and created opportunity.

Next, I had to take this progress from a group setting to an individual level if I really wanted to cement the relationship. This took some research. I knew that if I could figure out a way to reconnect with her, she would remember who I was, and if my message was compelling enough, I would build a one-on-one connection.

So I began my research. I was able to find the person who originally set up the event. I told her what my goal was and enlisted her to be part of my team, to help get me in a meeting. After a few attempts, I was able to obtain the sports legend's email address. The next step was to craft a compelling message.

I researched the individual. I watched documentaries on her and read articles. I learned as much as I could to determine where we had a connection and what would be in it for her to meet with me. In the middle of all this, I found out that her current employment was in jeopardy due to some staffing changes.

My strategy emerged: I was going to try to hire her.

Compiling all the research and identifying potential values, background, and aspirations, I crafted a message proposing for her to visit with me about how we could help her build her best life. My message was not general, but the specifics in it were a risk. If I had misjudged her values or mistaken her goals, I could have offended her or lost her attention.

Fortunately, I was accurate in my research and received a response. We scheduled an interview.

Now, I do hundreds of interviews a year and have done thousands in my career. I prepared more in-depth for this one than I ever have. I wrote and rewrote my questions and role-played with my wife. I made sure I was not going to waste one second of this person's time. I wanted to ensure that she felt as valued and important as she was in my eyes.

And then it happened—a sixty-minute meeting that stretched beyond two hours and went well. We connected. We laughed. We cried. We talked about the past, present, and future.

Ultimately, we were not a fit, but I did walk away with a new relationship. I believe she left very encouraged and validated, and I had an incredible experience. I believe knowing her will prove to be valuable for both parties in the future.

That is what it means to take a shot. It does not always go in. Sometimes you shoot an airball, and other times, it's a swish. As the phrase goes, "Nothing ventured, nothing gained." With many relationships, you never know where they could lead. But if they do lead somewhere, it will be exciting. Ultimately, they will amplify your capacity in ways you couldn't have even imagined, and you will find yourself living your best life!

Part 5: Breakthrough

As Joe awoke at 5:00 a.m., as usual, he instantly felt bad about the comments he had spewed toward his new bride the previous night. The weight of his remorse blanketed him as he sauntered down to a quiet area on the grass of the sprawling resort. It was still dark, and no one was around. Joe enjoyed this habit that he had established several months before after reading Hal Elrod's *Miracle Morning*. He began to go through his SAVERS routine:[7]

S—Silence

The noisy silence of his guilt was deafening. As Joe sat there, he did the only thing he knew to do: pray. He prayed for his marriage and that he would be filled with grace and love for Sarah. He prayed that he would be able to muster the humility to apologize. He prayed for the wisdom to know how to navigate this circumstance and be the husband he had always envisioned his future self being.

A—Affirmations

Joe repeated these affirmations to himself:

- "I am an incredible, loving husband."

---

7. Hal Elrod, *The Miracle Morning: The Not-So-Obvious Secret Guaranteed to Transform Your Life* (Before 8AM) (Hal Elrod International, Inc., 2012).

- "I have all the knowledge, skill, and wisdom I need to conquer today."

V—Vision

Joe recited a description of his self-proclaimed future: "I will leave a legacy of prosperity, wisdom, caring, and generosity toward my family. My grandchildren's grandchildren will know who I am and what I did for our family."

E—Exercise

He pumped out fifty jumping jacks, push-ups, and crunches.

R—Reading

Joe picked up his copy of *The Capacity Model* and opened it to his bookmark, staring squarely at chapter 12: "Personal Relationships." As he began to read, he quickly completed the section about how to grow his capacity by strengthening his relationship with his spouse.

Ouch.

S—Scribing

And finally, Joe jotted down some notes, finishing his Miracle Morning. He headed back toward his room, feeling rejuvenated and ready for a fresh start.

As he flashed his room key across the sensor, he heard the lock click open, and he twisted the doorknob. He burst through the door and saw Sarah sitting on the corner of the bed.

"I'm sorry!" poured out of both of their mouths simultaneously as they wrapped their arms around each other in a warm embrace.

Breakthrough.

Chapter 13: Closing Thoughts

Now we have arrived at the beginning. The beginning of an incredible journey. You now possess your new-found mindset—a place you can go to when life seems overwhelmingly stressful. Remember these two important truths about stress:

- Stress is a gift.
- Stress is life's natural gift telling you that it's time to grow.

What hours ago might have seemed like a horrible joke now is an empowering anthem to push you to new heights. When you slip into the trap of breakdown, you will have tools to consciously choose breakthrough.

The journey starts now with your ideal envisioned future state. Here is a series of questions covering five topics that can help you do a self-assessment to discover steps you can take to live your best life possible:

1. What does your best life look like? Write it down.

2. Now, rate yourself. On a scale of 1 to 7, where is your capacity ceiling each for your education, habits, and relationships?

3. Do you need to get additional formal education? How about informal? Which subjects and types would help you improve capacity?

4. How about your habits? Examine your being, relating, and doing habits. Where are you crushing it? Where would you like to improve?

5. Finally, look at your relationships. Do your professional relationships need more attention? Or are your personal relationships the ones that have been neglected?

Use these questions as a guide to determine what to focus on first. Pick the area that needs the most attention. Grab an idea from that section of the book and go to work.

Tell others you are working on it. Ask them if you can update them regularly. Give this book to a friend and ask him or her to read it so that person will know what you are talking about. Create a study group and work together to come up with an action plan to develop your capacity together.

Visit www.bestlife.builders for more tools and resources to help you along with this journey.

If we all would view stress through this positive lens, this world will be so much more enjoyable, and we would have more grace and understanding.

Our mistakes and shortcoming are just breakthrough stepping stones in building our capacity sky-high, handling stress, and building the best life possible!

Acknowledgments

Thank you to my friend and mentor, Reed, for inspiring me to do something big and write this book instead of getting my MBA.

Thank you to my editors—Elizabeth, Abigail, Nicole, and Libbye—for revising this book. My readers thank you for saving them from my first draft. I couldn't have done it without you.

Thank you, Nic and Chris, for keeping me accountable on progressing this book.

Thank you to my mom for encouraging me to start my first business and allowing me to run my dirty asphalt-seal-coating company out of your prized minivan and laundry room.

Thank you to my dad and granddad for your military service to this country and for pioneering the professional authorship legacy in the Perry Family.

Thank you to Rob for hiring me and taking a chance on a twenty-year-old kid. You helped start this journey.

About the Author

Steven Perry is a nationally recognized entrepreneur, leader, and motivator. He started his first business at age fifteen and entered the extremely challenging and rewarding field as a life insurance agent at age twenty. Five years later, he was promoted to partner in his local firm. He has been in executive leadership ever since.

Steven has received national recognition as a top performer in nearly every measurable performance category. He holds the distinction of winning more national trophies in a single year than anyone in his company's 175+ year history—twice in a row.

He has personally hired and led hundreds of growth-minded entrepreneurs and leaders and makes it his life's mission to "lead others into building their best lives."

Since 2011, Steven has been married to his beautiful wife, Tabatha, and they were blessed with daughters Lily (2014) and Liberty (2016). Originally from San Diego, California, Steve and Tabatha both lived in Alaska for more than twenty years.